"During the first years of my copywriting business, Maryclaire Collins was always a supportive colleague and a valuable source of industry know-how. Her book continues to provide me with hands-on practical knowledge and trade secrets."

> —JOHN M. MORA, John M. Mora Creative Communications, LaGrange, IL

"With her special gift for telling stories and painting pictures in her writing, Maryclaire adds an extra dimension to our corporate projects. Her readers will learn how they, too, might provide clients with detailed descriptions, colorful commentary and insightful perspective—in a clear, concise style."

> —HELEN RAECE WUERL, Manager, Public Relations, FMC Corporation

How to Make Money

Writing

Corporate

Communications

Maryclaire Collins

A PERIGEE BOOK

A Perigee Book
Published by The Berkley Publishing Group
200 Madison Avenue
New York, NY 10016

First edition: January 1995

Published simultaneously in Canada.

Library of Congress Cataloging-in-Publication Data

Collins, Maryclaire.
    How to make money writing corporate communications / by Maryclaire
Collins.
       p.   cm.
    "A perigee book."
    Includes bibliographical references.
    ISBN 0-399-51894-0
    1. Business writing—Vocational guidance.   2. Self-employed.
3. Small business—Management.   I. Title.
HF5718.3.C64   1995   94-3627
658.4'53—dc20   CIP

Printed in the United States of America

10 9 8 7 6 5 4 3 2 1

I dedicate this book to my husband, Jeff Lieberman.

Since we met, you have lovingly offered suggestions about my writing, my business, and my struggles. You continue to encourage me to take on new challenges—even if they disrupt our lives. I know I can always count on your advice to be consistent, objective, and honest—albeit sometimes painful. Thank you for being there when I need you.

SPECIAL THANKS

Many people contributed personal energy and extracurricular time to help me put together this book. I apologize if I have failed to mention anyone.

First, I must sing the praises of veteran published author Sue Sussman, who heard me lecture and urged me to turn my ideas into a book. She also passed on the phone number for her literary agent, Jane Jordan Browne, who took a chance on me, a book-publishing rookie. Eventually I had the pleasure of establishing a relationship with my editor at Perigee, Irene Prokop, who massaged, coaxed, and pummeled my book into shape.

Several other people helped me put meat on my book's bones. The Highland Park Public Library's reference librarians guided me to all the right sources for background. Kim Nauer, an up-and-coming Brooklyn free-lancer, expedited my survey of corporate communicators. My sharp, diplomatic client at the FMC Corporation, Helen Wuerl, offered her dependable opinions on what to include in that survey and generally encouraged my efforts. My husband's law firm, Barack, Ferrazzano, Kirschbaum & Perlman, welcomed me into its offices and loaned me a personal computer when mine failed. And Jim Ballard offered his photographic wizardry for my back-cover photo.

Then there are people who may not realize how much they contributed to my writing this book. My journalism professor, George Harmon, clued me into business writing and offered continuing advice about this business long after I graduated from

Northwestern University. And Dennis Wilcox, a former boss and colleague, taught me to intone the phrase *What am I trying to say here?* when I write.

Thanks also to several family members and friends, who graciously endured my gripes about juggling life and work. My sister, Katherine Collins Werner, did all that and reviewed the entire manuscript (on deadline)! My various running partners—Lorna Davis, Wendi Sloane Weitman, and Virginia Kelly—let me blow off steam on the trail. My mother, Florence Collins, encouraged me to keep travel and life journals and taught me to rewrite until my hands cramped. "It can always be better," she used to chirp as I hunched over my kitchen-table scribbling. And, my brother, Peter Thomas Collins, has always shared with me the magic and power of words and music.

And finally, my unskilled but loyal office staff, Paris and Gizmo, reliably glue themselves to my side and make sure no messenger escapes without at least fifty barks and a woof.

To all of you, I say many thanks!

Contents

Introduction

Whether you're a corporate free-lance writer already, or just toying with taking the plunge into this lucrative profession, this book will explain the ins and outs of how to market yourself and your writing services to corporate communications departments across the country. It will also guide you through the pitfalls and show you how to:

- Define your target companies
- Zero in on the right internal contacts
- Polish your portfolio
- Sell your services
- Negotiate your fees
- Navigate the corporate seas without making waves
- Maintain your corporate relationships to generate future work

Until now, there has not been a comprehensive book that can guide writers in marketing themselves directly to corporate communications and public relations departments. When I started my business in 1986, I was not able to find the information I needed, and other free-lancers were loath to spill any tips.

I knew from working inside a corporation that free-lancers regularly landed lucrative assignments writing newsletters, brochures, marketing magazines, corporate personnel newspapers, benefits communiqués, speeches, and video scripts. As a senior editor in the communications department of a large insurance company, I collaborated with and negotiated fees with free-lance writers, sometimes known as "contract writers." This gave me a client-side perspective on this writers' market as well as an understanding of the dynamics of the corporate relationships freelancers develop with their internal corporate clients.

I also observed firsthand that they were making better money and enjoying greater personal and professional freedom than I was as a corporate flack punching a time clock. I mulled over what I would miss besides the steady paycheck and insurance safety net if I, too, took the plunge. What did I have to lose, except:

- Filling out time sheets
- Dealing with office politics
- Groveling for raises
- Begging for good assignments
- Paying my corporate political dues
- Clearing my desk daily (allowing six "personal" items like a telephone)
- Attending pointless meetings
- Sharing a computer
- Dressing up every day
- Restraining my rather exuberant personal style

It would be an understatement to say that I was *not* a natural corporate type! Conflict accessorized my work life. Free-lancing seemed like my ticket out.

As a rookie with only some clips, a résumé, and some insider information, I thought I knew the ropes. But surprises awaited me. In order to succeed, I had to master many aspects of free-lancing, including how to:

- Familiarize myself with many industries
- Set up an appropriate computer system
- Create a knockout portfolio
- Cold call comfortably
- Wade through corporate structures
- Identify communications decision-makers
- Follow up on marketing calls

- Cultivate internal contacts
- Follow up with clients for postmortems
- Discipline myself
- Design short- and long-term strategies for my business

In a calculated effort to leverage my insurance writing experience, I first went after financial and insurance institutions. Later on, I tried my luck with completely different industries and randomly targeted new companies.

With the Yellow Pages and several trade association directories in hand, I experimented with cold calling. It wasn't as tough as I expected, and the approach paid off. Six weeks after beginning my search, I landed my first assignments with two Fortune 500 companies. Pretty soon, one assignment spawned another and my portfolio swelled. As each client perused my recent clips from other companies, the work avalanched.

To this day, I can be as busy as I want to be, if I'm willing to hunker down to the telephone, crank out letters, leave voice mail messages, and keep pumping out quality work for my clients.

In my first year as a free-lancer, 1986–1987, I more than matched my previous corporate salary. In subsequent years I either doubled or tripled that figure. And I've done it working on average about fifteen hours a week. Granted, some weeks I work sixty hours on client assignments, and other weeks I work only four hours, mostly on marketing calls and letters. The rest of the time I train for marathons, take voice lessons or go to the zoo with my kids.

With very little continuing effort, you too can tap the corporate writing market and rake in a terrific income if you latch onto a successful, flexible formula for marketing yourself.

As you test your mettle in this free-lance arena, you'll find that you need to bend and flex your strategies to accommodate each company and every internal client you work with in that company. Surviving and thriving in this business is as much a matter of getting along with people as it is a matter of being a good writer.

That's not to say that I ignore writing quality. On the contrary, regularly churning out clean, grammatical, entertaining copy is what earns you new clients, keeps long-term clients happy, and generates referrals.

Success in this business is also about staying on top of the latest technology that might offer you access to new assignments, higher-quality work product, greater versatility, and more services for your clients.

You might wonder about starting such a business while the economy is still digging out from a recession. I can't count how many people have quizzed me about how I've maintained my business throughout the recession of the last few years. In response to these inquiries, I somewhat sarcastically refer to myself as a "bottom feeder."

In other words, when a company has downsized its communications departments, opportunities arise for me. Maybe not immediately, as the department takes stock and sets a new course for the future, but soon enough, several things occur to the benefit of a free-lancer.

Even after a company cannot afford to pay for the in-house personnel's salary and related benefits costs, that company still needs to get the word out about corporate activities and upcoming changes. Who will handle the flood of critical communications needs before and long after the downsizing goes into effect?

This is one of the many times when companies might call on a free-lancer's services.

Management realizes it needs to circle the wagons and loop arms tightly with the employees who survived the downsizing, to refocus employees' attention on the future and not on whether they're possibly getting the axe. To accomplish this, management has to communicate the reconfigured company's new direction couched in encouraging, inspirational, and morale-boosting words. And, if they've set adrift a boatload of communications department refugees, then they'll still need somebody on board to get out the messages.

That someone can be you, the free-lance writer.

Fewer internal people to fulfill more communications needs spells greater opportunity for free-lancers. And now, as companies' bottom lines improve with a more buoyant economy, and more communicators return to new and perhaps cushier offices, my business volume continues to grow.

During a go-go period, businesses are more willing to invest in more experimental and sophisticated communications as well as longer-term projects that might otherwise sit on the back burner. My experience has been that in good times and bad, there's work out there for the enterprising writer.

I base most of my advice on my personal free-lance experiences. So, for a slightly different perspective—the client's—take a look at the first appendix, which includes the results of an unscientific but broadly based survey I conducted with in-house corporate communicators, mostly from my Chicago home base. To elicit their cooperation and candid responses, I agreed not to identify any individual company by name. It's refreshing to see what they have to say about free-lancers and what they expect from them.

So if you have the appetite for nurturing business relationships, selling yourself on the phone and via letters, communicating with flair and running a business, then you have a great head start in corporate communications free-lancing.

Chapter I

The Successful
Start-Up

The happy free-lancer is the one who can't keep up with the workload.

Before you launch into the free-lance corporate writing world, take stock of your motivations, experience, skills, goals, and entrepreneurial aptitude. Basically, you need to decide if you have what it takes to succeed at this business. In addition, you need to look at your current professional status and decide if it is indeed a good time for you to make the switch, to plunge into a new endeavor.

You will be able to make such a decision by analyzing your strengths and gauging your readiness and aptitude for this adventure. At the end of the chapter, I've included a lighthearted self-test that delves into some personal and professional dilemmas faced daily by corporate free-lancers.

Start with do-it-yourself analysis. It's cheaper than the real kind, but it's just as essential to keeping your feet on the ground if you plan to take on the corporate world as a free-lance writer. Many people erroneously believe that starting a free-lance writing business of any sort merely means you need a good word processor and a dedicated phone line. Actually, a lot of nonwriting and other often invisible variables profoundly influence your business and can stunt your tenure as a free-lancer.

So, do some soul-searching to arm yourself with a critical but respectful eye for your particular skills, weaknesses, and natural work-style inclinations. Remember that everyone who does succeed at this business comes to it with different levels of talent and awareness. Understand that, and begin tallying what things *you* need to learn, change or purchase to make this job work for you. Kick off this process by addressing the following:

1. Assess Your Current Writing Skills

Even if you have not been a *professional* writer before, you may still have what it takes to be a free-lance corporate writer. Don't be put off by seasoned or cynical pros who might have an ulterior motive for discouraging a newcomer to the corporate writing world.

When you look at your skills, take into account how many jobs or educational adventures have required you to write or communicate. All this adds to your skills repertoire, as chronicled by your portfolio. (Look at #7, "Portfolio Power," in this chapter.) Ask yourself these questions:

- Have you always enjoyed writing?
- When you were a student, did you look forward to writing papers?
- Have you written for newspapers or magazines professionally?
- Have employers or teachers complimented your writing?
- Do you have any experience with public relations work?
- Did you study journalism or public relations in college or graduate school?
- Do you have problems with spelling or grammar? Or have you always had a facility for language and did you excel at spelling tests as a kid?
- Is it easiest for you to understand a concept after you've written it down?
- Did you write for your high school or college newspapers?

2. Rate Your Personality

Many different people succeed at free-lancing for corporations. And no one personality can hit it off with all those companies and their internal people. So, in a way, it doesn't matter whether you're quiet, boisterous, serious or eccentric. What does matter is how you get along with other people.

Many client respondents to the survey I sent out (see Appendix I) named personality as one of the top three criteria for sustaining an ongoing relationship with a given corporate client. Apparently it might pay to do a little soul-searching about your interpersonal skills.

Think about your past work experiences. Did you ever have personality conflicts with coworkers or bosses? Did you find it easy to take orders, work in teams, negotiate salaries or job responsibilities? In a job interview, what three words would you use to describe your strengths? Your weaknesses? How do you take criticism? Do you like being the boss? How do you feel about consulting colleagues about decisions or projects?

Keep in mind that free-lancing is an unpredictable livelihood, demanding flexibility and versatility, both professionally and personally. You will deal with many different people, new assignments, changing job responsibilities, varying office environments, and deadlines all the time. And that might be within just one company.

So perhaps a roll-with-the-punches approach to life would be a good personality anchor for a free-lancer. But it would be only one of many assets a free-lancer should hone when launching a corporate writing business.

3. Evaluate Your Goals and Ambitions

In many job interviews and on résumés, people talk about or write down their specific job objectives. It's just as important to analyze your motivations for free-lancing as well.

Think about what initially inspired you to consider corporate free-lancing. Did you fall into it by happenstance? Did you lose your internal corporate spot? Is this just a hobby you want to try out? Are you a former consumer press writer who wants to try the public relations and internal corporate route in your own business?

People from numerous backgrounds become corporate free-lancers: fiction writers, marketing communications people, copy-writers, moonlighting newspaper reporters, graphics designers who have a way with words, downsized corporate communicators, entrepreneurial types who can't hack a corporate structure, and people who just plain want to work from home.

I've met people with many different rationales for starting a free-lance business, and with just as many long- and short-term ambitions for that business. For several years during the sluggish, downsizing late 1980s, I contended that laid-off in-house corporate communicators would flood the free-lance arena. Some did, but to my surprise I have run into only a few who opted to stick with the business long-term.

Although they were terrific communicators and writers, many of them weren't too comfortable or adept with marketing. Others merely preferred the security of a full-time job and banked on companies recalling them when the economy recovered. They played the odds correctly. Gloria Gordon, a vice president of communications with the International Association of Business Communicators (IABC), contends that the trend has already come full circle.

"We're seeing lots of new 'old' faces returning to our association's ranks, as companies are hiring back the people they let go," says Gordon. "This has two effects on free-lancers. Either it means there won't be any work left for them at those companies, or the company will have even more work for everyone."

Basically, as you analyze your goals and free-lance ambitions, think about how committed you are to the concept of free-lancing. Then envision how your business might and will change in five, ten, or fifteen years. Is this just a stopgap measure until you find another full-time spot, or, for instance, do you project this one-person business expanding someday into a public relations agency?

4. Assess Your Lifestyle

Life as a free-lancer is quite unpredictable, both professionally and personally. While we've talked about flexibility on the job as being a key anchor for success with clients, it's just as important on the home front.

Do you like a predictable nine-to-five work schedule that doesn't interfere with after-work racquetball appointments, evening grocery shopping, and Saturday doctors' appointments for the kids? Do you like to count on a biweekly paycheck, two weeks off for vacation annually, sick days when you need them, and health insurance paid mostly by your employer? If so, you may have a tough time dealing with the odd schedule, financial ups and downs, and go-it-alone life of a free-lancer.

I've found over the years that free-lancing has been a series of feasts followed by brief, but disturbing, famines. For two weeks, I might put in 120 hours on three client projects, then work only about 15 hours the following two weeks, on administrative catch-up work. Or, I might receive two $5,000 checks from clients one week, only to see an empty mailbox for a month. Or, I find myself waking at three every morning one week in order to make phone calls to Pakistan for interviews. Or, I have to delay filing a quarterly estimated tax payment until a client invoice is paid.

Do these kinds of situations cause your heart to palpitate? If so, turn back now, reread *Dress for Success,* brush up your interviewing skills and résumé, and get back into the full-time corporate employment racket.

The above-mentioned reality checks are only a small part of the chaos that can accompany free-lancing. If your office is at home, which for most free-lancers is the case, then you might also have to deal with making your professional life coexist amicably with your at-home personal life. That can be tough.

If you have to call Brussels from Chicago before the workday ends there, be ready to make those phone calls while your kids pitch Eggos across the breakfast table at each other, the dogs pace in front of the back door, or your neighbor upstairs rockets into a high-impact Salsarobics class for a little eye-opener.

Oh, the variety and spice of a free-lancing life is not for everyone! And it's best to be forewarned of the downside.

5. Gauge Your Attitude Toward Work in General

Think about the ways in which you work best. Think about the environment that makes you most productive. Is it the library, a bustling newsroom, a quiet nook under the first-floor staircase, or in front of the 10 P.M. news? Can you work just about anywhere when you know you have to meet a deadline?

What kind of attitude do you bring to any work? Are you a procrastinator? Do you like a lot of support in researching assignments? Or do you like playing Sherlock Holmes and hunting down information yourself?

Successful free-lancers share a few common characteristics when it comes to work attitude. They're self-starters and they meet deadlines. And if they're particularly ambitious about sustaining a profitable business, they're hustlers. They spend some quality time doing marketing and following up with existing and potential clients.

Larry Robbins, director of the communications program at the Wharton School, University of Pennsylvania, estimates that free-lancers probably should spend about 40 percent of their time on marketing. Would you be comfortable doing that?

6. Check Your Entrepreneurial Aptitude

Part of a free-lancer's hustling attitude comes inborn with an entrepreneur's genetic makeup. Some people are naturally good at selling themselves. Others aren't. If you're serious about free-lancing, then buff up your business skills.

Are you single-mindedly compelled to jump-start a business? Are you hungry, or just muddling around with free-lancing for distraction? Does the idea of rustling up business on the phone and actually getting a hit give you an endorphin rush? Do you sometimes dream what it would be like to nurture a one-person business into a major public relations and communications firm?

Does the idea of getting turned down by one prospect only make you want to try five new prospects? Are you ready to set up a word processing station with a fax/modem, to install a second and third phone line, to arrange a separate tax accounting system, to learn a new graphics program, to take a speech-writing seminar?

In addition, do you think you have what it takes to set up a service business? It doesn't matter whether it's free-lancing, hair-styling, legal work, or voice coaching—do some homework and find out what you need to do to make it work, to market your services, to build a book of business, and to become profitable. Free-lance corporate writing is no different.

7. Portfolio Power

A writer's portfolio is a key sales tool. In the process of tracking down and tapping the free-lance corporate market, you will most likely have to show prospects some writing samples, which are evidence of your professional writing ability. Whether sent by mail or presented in person, your samples package represents you in many subtle and not-so-subtle ways. Because of this, you'll want to organize examples of your best work in one elegant, simple, but power-packed collection.

If you have many different media represented in your samples, then you will need a fairly large case for presentation. I recommend a professional-looking case made for this purpose, rather than any loose-leaf container or paper envelope of copies. A case is sturdier, easier to transport, and will protect your valuable sample works for minimal cost.

How it looks on the outside is important: It tangibly represents you, your creativity, your professionalism, organization, and conscientiousness. A flimsy, torn, or tacky portfolio might tell a prospect something else.

Portfolio cases can be bought at art supply, luggage, and stationery stores. They do not have to be leather; many of the vinyl cases are tasteful and far less expensive. For a vinyl case, as wide as a standard briefcase and slightly taller, you might spend anywhere from $30 to $125. The portfolio should be deep enough to hold one or two videotapes as well as several dozen print samples inserted into clear plastic sleeves held inside the portfolio's binder or spine.

Some writers opt for loose plastic sleeves, but I prefer portfolios with bound plastic sleeves to control the order of my samples. While other free-lancers might keep their samples uncovered inside a portfolio, I adopted the policy long ago of protecting my samples at all costs from dirty fingers, food spills, and the ravages of age. It can prove difficult and sometimes impossible to obtain additional copies of work from some clients, so treasure the originals.

I recommend buying a case that zips (easily!) all the way around and can open out flat when unzipped. Open the different types at the store and inspect them. Try to be objective and consider how a new client will look at the portfolio for the first time in a presentation.

When you pack up the case for presentation, you will want to visibly display the originals with some copies underneath that you can give to the prospective client. Pick these pieces and order them strategically according to who will view them at a presentation. Each prospect deserves a customized version of that portfolio. You must be ready to re-sort the portfolio for perusal according to the nature of the client's business or the specific assignments dished out to free-lancers. There is no one-size-fits-all here. Try to include samples that:

- You wrote about that industry
- Are germane to the company's new products or services
- You wrote for a competitor
- Feature current economic/business issues

Assembling your work into an effective portfolio presentation requires you to objectively sift through your "clips" and "archive" them for the future. Clips can be any writing samples, but the word typically refers to published articles that you have torn out of a newspaper or magazine. Archiving them means you'll save those original samples, and make multiple, readable, 8.5″ × 11″ copies of each. Stick with this standard size to ease your prospect's review of your work; larger copies mean the client may have to unfold something in order to read it.

Look at all the articles, brochures, scripts, advertisements, training materials, speeches, and so on, that you've written. Organize them to emphasize the ones that were produced professionally. Yes, any that you produced for college or graduate school assignments or college newspapers are important—if they're the only clips you have. But published clips increase your credibility with future corporate clients and stamp your portfolio with a professional luster.

Many times, new free-lancers have forgotten how many assignments they have completed over the years. Dig back into your memory banks. Perhaps you were a stringer for a local paper, wrote a brochure for your sister's new business while you were in college, or ghostwrote a friend's Rotary Club speech. These are all legitimate clips for a free-lancer's portfolio. Look through old boxes stored in your attic, or hunt through your word processor's directories and files.

If you have a handful of these professional originals, great! At this point, don't worry about when you completed these assignments. Just be glad you've got some samples at all. And, remember, most potential clients reviewing your samples aren't going to carbon date them. They want to see how you write. The fact that the speech or brochure was written three years ago doesn't really matter.

What does matter is that you can honestly present your samples as yours. Clients understand the role of an editor in producing any company publications or PR materials. However, if your sample doesn't even slightly resemble the original you gave to the editor involved in the project, then pitch it. It's not your sample anymore—it's the editor's.

If you must send samples in the mail, be sure you keep copies and enclose a self-addressed, stamped envelope for their return by first-class mail. Include a cover letter, résumé, and client list (if possible). The return envelope will encourage the recipient to drop the samples in the mail, and the postage will ensure that your valuable clips don't fall victim to the fourth-class rate.

The F.A.T. (Collins's Free-Lance Aptitude Test)

In this chapter I've given you an idea of what you need to think about before starting up a free-lance writing business for corporations. Now you can take this test and see where you fall on my free-lance aptitude scale. (No, you don't need a No. 2 pencil to complete this.)

Free-lancers come in all shapes and sizes, but many share some key characteristics professionally and personally that seem to make them more successful than others. More than anything, this little test should jog your mind about what parts of your work attitude and skills are weak or strong.

A) When you're on deadline, working in your home office, would you pick up the home phone line if you heard it ringing?

1. of course, I wouldn't miss personal calls during the day
2. probably
3. only if expecting a call
4. probably not
5. not on your life

B) How do you feel after billing a seventy-hour week, knowing that you don't have another assignment pending for a couple weeks?

1. terrific, I finally get some time off
2. pretty good, but a little worried
3. fairly concerned about no follow-up work
4. losing sleep and dreaming about clients
5. frantically doing marketing calls

C) When you drive your family car for business, how do you like to track your mileage?

1. I ballpark my annual mileage.
2. I estimate my mileage, usually quarterly.
3. I try to tally it based on date book entries.
4. I usually track it in a ledger weekly.
5. I fanatically jot it down each time in a ledger—complete with date, business purpose, and destination.

D) Free-lancing is a great career alternative for a loner.

1. definitely
2. probably
3. sometimes

4. probably not
5. definitely not

E) Corporations aren't trying to put a newspaper out every day, so their deadlines for free-lancers are or should be pretty elastic.

1. agree—what's the big deal?
2. agree generally
3. agree a little
4. disagree generally
5. disagree wholeheartedly

F) If your writing skills need a little brushup, would you be willing to invest in a writing workshop, take an internship, or read some guides on writing?

1. I figure I'll learn on the job.
2. I'd like to but don't have time.
3. I might consider it.
4. I'd try at least one option.
5. I'd start with some guides and try to take a night course.

G) If your office phone rings at 2 A.M., and you know it's an overseas source for a project, what do you do?

1. throw the phone across the room
2. pretend to be my message machine when I realize it's a source
3. answer and reschedule
4. answer, slosh through the interview, and go back to sleep
5. guzzle a cup of preprogrammed coffee and interview the source with a song in my heart

H) "The client is always right."

1. rarely, that's why they need my help
2. sometimes, but I make sure they understand my side
3. generally, but I let them know when they're not
4. absolutely, even when I disagree

I) After five rejections during cold calls one afternoon, I feel

1. encouraged that delivering pizza can earn me $4.85 per hour
2. disappointed, and don't do any more for the week
3. concerned about the effectiveness of my marketing
4. disappointed, but maybe try a few more
5. determined to persevere and make five more calls

J) This is what I do when house chores, like buying dog food or doing laundry, hover over me:

1. I take care of them to avoid my writing.
2. I complete them first thing every morning before I start writing.
3. I complete essential personal chores during the workday.
4. I make my spouse/mate/partner/dog do them.
5. I save them for the weekends.

K) I want to be a free-lancer because

1. I'm a recluse and don't like people or work.
2. I haven't been able to find full-time work for years.
3. It sounds different and might be fun.
4. I don't like working for somebody else and I love having my office at home.
5. I'm a writer and I've always wanted to have my own business.

Add up your answers from the numbers that precede your chosen responses. The bigger the number the better.

If your total falls between 11 and 22, I'd say you better think about a different profession. If your total falls between 23 and 44, you've definitely got potential as a free-lancer. If your total falls between 45 and 55, then I'm shaking in my boots fearing that you might move to Chicago and pirate away my clientele.

Chapter II

Brush Up on the Basics

Many IN-HOUSE corporate communicators complain that they see a lack of solid journalistic skills in the work product or samples of free-lance writers—particularly new ones. While this chapter may be unnecessary for some writers, I believe the issue of sloppy writing skills merits some discussion.

When I mentioned I was working on this book to George Harmon, one of my former professors at Northwestern University's Medill School of Journalism, he suggested that I include a chapter outlining the basics of good writing.

"So many people get out there in the corporate world, and they can't put sentences and paragraphs together coherently or grammatically," said Harmon, the director of Medill's economics and business writing degree program. "There's too much bad writing going around. Maybe after people leave an academic environment they get sloppy and forget what's supposed to be right."

You might have the marketing skills of a Dale Carnegie graduate, but if you can't write clearly and grammatically, you won't last in the free-lance corporate writing business.

Correct information, grammar, punctuation, and spelling form the core of solid writing. It's not sexy stuff. But these skills go a long way toward cementing enduring relationships with clients. And while it's great to infuse your writing with some bite and cleverness, they merely add the foam to the cappuccino.

What Do Clients Expect?

Although it's difficult to assess up front exactly what grammar style satisfies any in-house editor, you won't go wrong if you stick with fundamentals, at least initially.

Many companies structure their own stringent publication standards and stylebook preferences to which free-lancers and in-house writers must adhere. If you can look at internal publications prior to soliciting work from a company, all the better. Then you can analyze what an editor considers perfect, final copy. That should be your guide in all your writing for that company. (See Chapter IX, "Now That You're the Hired Gun.") Short of that, editors will just want to see a grammatical, error-free writing style from you. They may understand departures from their own idiosyncratic style preferences, if you're consistent.

One of my clients insists that I capitalize all personnel titles and department names, regardless of where they appear. Another client always uses first names in quote attributions, once I spell out the source's full name on first mention. Although this departs from my benchmark style bible, *The Associated Press Stylebook,* I respect my clients' wishes. And I assume this departure won't cause me to be turned away from the Pearly Grammar Gates and plunged into Punctuation Purgatory.

On the other hand, if you're still not absolutely clear on how to punctuate quotes, how to choose correct possessives, or when to use "there" versus "their," you have some work ahead of you.

Clients hire outside free-lance writers to minimize their workload. They don't want to spend any extra time tidying up a writer's spelling, grammar, and clarity problems. Writers jeopardize their credibility, value, and longevity with clients if they don't fulfill these basic needs.

You Are What You Write

I contend that lawyers churn out some mighty confusing, convoluted writing. And when I have quizzed a few of them about this—the marathon run-on sentences, the stilted language, the constant repetition of specific terms, clauses, names—they have indignantly replied this is all for the sake of clarity. *Clarity!* Call me stupid, but I have never waded through a contract without being stumped by what many paragraphs intended to say.

OK, lawyers shouldn't shoulder all the blame for the world's lack of clear writing. Many top-notch professionals of every stripe have trouble making themselves understood on paper, especially in an entertaining, clear fashion.

Work-world insiders cultivate, spew forth, and encourage sins of the printed word. And it's not just bad grammar and poor spelling that lie at the root of consistently bad writing. Jargon, knowledge assumption, poor organization, and deadly verbiage all can wilt and obscure an intended written message. They aren't technical writing violations, necessarily, but in the business world they certainly won't help promote the product, service, or action that a company is bothering to write about.

Think about your own professional background and what types of writing you have done over the years. Then think about how this background might have handicapped your ability to write clear, grammatical, and fresh prose. Many people blindly ignore their ingrained poor writing habits. They're tough to break.

Did you work for a pharmaceutical company that had you write up new-product specification sheets? Are you from the academic world and inclined to writing long-winded, theoretical analyses? Are you a former advertising copywriter who has trouble writing anything with more flow than a brochure?

Even if you are confident you can adapt your writing style to each corporate client's specifications, be prepared to review the client's previously published or recorded works. At least this will ready you to field his or her questions about your writing's suitability for that particular communications environment.

Once You're In

With the first few assignments, you should start incorporating the company's style into your first drafts. Remember that anything you write for a client (even scripts, which aren't a final product) requires vigilant attention to all style details. So try to proof your copy several times and aim for perfect first drafts.

A slightly different challenge occurs when your client's writing aptitude and editing aren't up to par. Try to observe discreetly which grammar rules he or she breaks unwittingly and compare those to the corporate-wide "house" style. Although most editors I've worked with have been grammar gurus and stellar writers, I have come across a few grammar busters.

The categories following this section merely touch on some key areas that every writer should master. I also mention some of the grammar errors that make me cringe when I read them. Rest assured, I don't intend this to replace the invaluable dictionaries, reference guides, and stylebooks that every writer should own. I am far from being a grammar maven, so I rely on these texts to resolve any questions I may have. (See Appendix II for suggested guides.)

Structure

Structure alone probably contributes more than anything else to a written communication's overall impact, quality, and effectiveness. No matter how beautiful the prose or convincing the facts, you must order a written piece so that it makes sense and conveys your intended messages accurately. My structural and clear-writing rules of thumb for many print communications are as follows:

- Write a lead or thesis first to help organize the rest of the writing.
- Use subheads to divide up longer pieces into digestible sections.
- Keep sentences short.
- Keep paragraphs short (three to five sentences is plenty).
- Trim excess adjectives/adverbs.
- Rely on action verbs for "zing."

One good way to ensure that your writing flows logically and meaningfully is to write an outline. Before writing an outline or first draft, I quickly list the high points I plan to address. Next to each point, I write down the names of the critical players or products involved. In addition I might jot down some cogent quotes I recall from actual interviews.

After this brainstorm, I reorder these high points, beginning with the most important information. I sometimes work directly from this list or use it as a basis for a more formal outline. Eventually the full quotes and factual data substantiate each of your high points and put the meat on a communications piece's skeleton.

Winging it by just dashing off a first draft doesn't always work, especially if the subject is highly technical or involves many different people, disciplines, or departments within the corporation.

Clean Leads

These help structure an article, signal what's to come, and hook the reader. They work in consumer journalism, and they work equally well in corporate newsletters and marketing magazines. Consider the lead a thesis statement that identifies the who, what, when, where, why, and how involved.

Even if I'm writing some other type of communications material—script, brochure, speech—I still formulate a lead in my head that guides me throughout the assignment. The same fundamentals applicable to a news article lead will offer structure, focus, and balance to all my other communications pieces. And although you don't write a "lead" for a brochure, you may come up with a teaser slogan that sums up the benefits and characteristics of some product, service, or company.

My rationale for this approach is that if I can't nail down these basics up front, my writing will ramble. If I skip this step and attempt to jump into a long (anything greater than fifteen hundred words) piece headlong, I could be asking for trouble. Sometimes I'm lucky and all the information falls into place, but only if I have absorbed a significant amount of it and have carved out a clear structure for the piece in my head.

If I wing it, and the information is new to me or the message's objective eludes me, I could spend extra time at the end reorganizing. That's precious time that's paid for by my client. I can't afford to allow that to happen.

Instead, I try to construct a lead that guides the entire communication. Then, I string that who-what-when-where-why-how information together coherently and build in the following critical objective: why the reader can't live without knowing the forthcoming information. Granted, there are many possible ways to begin a piece—a delayed lead; a quote lead; a catchy, abrupt quip; a question—but this should give you a start.

Subheads

These teaser subheadings serve to divide up a piece into more digestible parts for you and a reader or video audience. I like to use these in many different communications pieces, including brochures, articles, scripts, white papers, and pamphlets. Some clients request subheads in communications, while others may not use subheads at all. In that case, I might include them anyway for my own organizational purposes. Often I find that clients like them enough to retain them in the final piece.

I aim for clever subheads with a twist where appropriate. Otherwise I stick to straightforward, but always short, teasers of about two or three words. I sometimes call subheads teasers when they cleverly signal what's coming without revealing the most critical piece of information. Sometimes I manipulate key words of the main subject areas or I pull out catchy phrases from someone's quote.

In a newsletter or magazine article, I like to drop in subheads no more frequently than about every six or seven paragraphs. Otherwise they become a distraction and disjoint the writing. If possible, I try to make sure the previous paragraph has some transitional material in it, even if flimsy, that leads fairly smoothly into the next subgroup of information.

You have a little more latitude with a subhead's structure in brochures. They can vary in length quite a bit from one-word exclamations to short, catchy sentences that introduce upcoming material.

Make sure the subheads serve a function. Use them as an organizational device that also magnetizes the reader into wanting to continue finding out more about the subject discussed. Short pieces might not require them.

Keep Sentences Short

Complex sentences can confuse and diffuse unless they are flawlessly constructed. Danger lies ahead for the grammatically challenged writer whose sentences encompass more than one key subject-and-verb structure. While I don't suggest adopting a "See Jane run" and "Go Spot go" style of writing, I do recommend breaking up long sentences into smaller units of information. This style eases the reader's burden, translates well into script-writing and brochure style, and keeps the writer on a logical organizational track. Doing this also makes it easier for the writer to monitor correct subject-verb agreement within each sentence.

When I coach businesspeople who want to sharpen their writing skills or style I start at this point. Too often when a businessperson tries to reconstruct a concept on paper, he or she will take an academic approach in the writing. After I analyze businesspeople's sentence structures with them, I ask them to talk to me about the particular subject the way they might explain it to a new colleague. I jot down their verbatim explanations, distill some of the key points, and then read what I have back to them.

I often start out by saying something like "Here's how I might write that first paragraph dealing with the new product roll-out . . ." Afterward they typically respond: "That's it, let me see what you wrote." Then I point out that I merely wrote down the words they used to explain the subject. Their conversational versions usually lack the highfalutin, complex language that people latch onto when writing about their ideas.

Even professional free-lancers benefit from stepping back from their writing and reading it out loud or just talking about the subject before putting anything on paper. I often spot-check the clarity of sentences longer than about thirty words with this technique. Sentences form links from one concept to another. If they're not clear, meaningful, and grammatical, they can jeopardize the entire written piece's coherence and structure.

Keep Paragraphs Short

Paragraph separations break up chunks of information while visually signaling that something related, but new and different, is coming. When a paragraph exceeds about six sentences, it's time to think about splitting it up.

I try to stick by this rule of thumb, regardless of what I write for my clients. Connecting one rambling sentence after another into one paragraph does not improve a message's impact. Keep paragraphs between three and five sentences if possible. This pertains to brochures and management letters as well as newsletter and magazine articles and white papers, those lengthier treatises a corporation might produce on specific topics in which it has expertise.

Trim Away Excess

Adverbs and adjectives should serve a specific purpose if you use them in business communications. Unless you have to describe the idyllic pastoral setting for some company's new factory, avoid too much editorializing through "ly" words and excessive adjectives.

Let the facts speak for themselves, and use quotes and crisp language for impact. If something is "extremely" or "very" critical to a company's operations, cut out the "extremely" or "very" and instead let a list of specific "whys" make that clear. (My junior-year high school English teacher would keel over if she discovered I ever use the word "very".)

Action Verbs for Zing

Liven up your writing anytime by hunting for energetic verbs and eliminating as many "to be" constructions from your sentences as you can. Corporate people fill their business writing with "to be" constructions and passive tenses, which disembody the writing, removing it from the message and the people involved. Instead of saying "the ditch machinery is turned on by on-site operators," try writing "the ditch machinery hums into action as operators flip ten switches." I have discovered that sometimes people generating corporate messages choose the "to be" route to avoid indicating a party responsible for a given action. Many times, however, people use it because they didn't bother to think of an alternative.

It's easier to use action verbs when you can identify a *person* as your subject in any sentence. Things don't just happen in companies. *People* make them happen. But all too often I'll read corporate copy that relies on people-less information. If I'm involved with a corporate writing project, I try to nail down specific people involved—the generators of ideas, changes, actions, operations, duties, and responsibilities within any company. Sooner or later, someone will surface as the generator. Once you identify those people, then you have an easier time choosing and using verbs that bite and compel.

I make this a mission with every writing assignment, even with the most stubborn, negative messages that seem to lack a human connection. If I have to use a "to be" construction, I do it with my head held high, knowing I tried to dig up an alternative. All facetiousness aside, the "to be" construction serves a function in the English language, and I use its different forms when necessary. I just avoid letting it become a crutch.

Stylebooks and Self-Editing

Rely on these for success with any writing and client. No one person can remember all the rules of grammar and punctuation. And no one reference book lists all the answers. I believe in consulting several guides or stylebooks on points of grammar. Typically I will defer to *Merriam-Webster's Collegiate Dictionary* or *The Associated Press Stylebook* if I find conflicting recommendations.

Consult reference guides as part of the self-editing process. Every writer struggles to be objective about his or her writing. Increased objectivity is born of skepticism and humility. The more you scour away weakness, error, and ambiguity from your writing, the better your final product. Scrupulous self-editing is natural to writers who realize they're human and can make mistakes. Your guiding motto should be: Polish, polish, polish.

Chapter III

The Art of Working at Home

Probably a free-lancer's final consideration before launching a business is deciding where to work and setting up that work-space environment for optimal productivity, comfort, and tax-purpose exclusivity. Don't assume you can plop a typewriter on the dining room table and call that your "office."

Everyone works differently. And different environments can evoke different behaviors and productivity levels even in one person. Your working environment can profoundly affect your free-lance success.

Some people thrive on a noisy, newsroom-style atmosphere and find their homes too quiet for them to work well. Others are distracted by a pin dropping and need a completely removed office space. Still others can crank out fabulous copy while three kids make dynamite in the kitchen.

Try to diagnose which workplace environment detracts from or improves your free-lance productivity. Then, when you decide to set up shop, seriously consider these questions:

- Do external noises or goings on easily distract you?
- Do you like puttering around the house—doing dishes, walking the dogs, answering the house phone?
- Do you like volunteering for car pools, kids' school projects, extracurricular hobbies?
- Do you like to keep your work life completely separate from your personal life?

- Do you mind having your work life overlap somewhat with home life?
- How seriously do you take your work?
- Do you have midday obligations requiring you to be at home or accessible to family members?
- Do you have pets that need daytime care?

If you decide to home-base your business, mull over the following considerations that can affect your workdays:

1. Do you have small children at home?

Seasoned professional writers of any sort will probably have a few post-college years under their belts. As you accumulate those birthdays, you might attach yourself somewhat permanently to other humans and possibly even a few kids along the way. Yes, even dedicated writers turn off the computer once in a while to break for some human contact.

Anyone working full- or even part-time outside the home has someone else care for his or her preschool-age kids. When you decide to work at home, the thought might cross your mind that you won't need child caretakers anymore.

Stop and think for a minute how that scenario might unfold. There you are juggling the colicky baby, phone calls from clients, the Federal Express pickups, phone interviews with sources, the laundry, the park visits, the peanut butter and jelly lunches, library research, diaper changes, the play group, the grocery shopping, the proofreading, and the inconsistent nap schedules. I tried it—for about two minutes.

I'm amazed at the starry-eyed glaze that comes over some people when they hear I work at home. They comment how idyllic it is that I can work and be with my kids at the same time. And then I pop that bubble and tell them I have a babysitter *and* an after-care arrangement for my other child when school is out.

I've learned that I can't parent well and take care of business appropriately at the same time. It's not fair to my kids or my business.

2. Is your living space big enough to accommodate office space?

Most of us can set aside a separate space at home for an office. Even the tiniest studio apartment has room for a desk that can accommodate a computer and phone, a chair, and a bookcase for references, supplies, and a printer. The question is: Can *you* work that way?

I carved out my first home office in the one-bedroom apartment I shared with my mate. It was interesting to work in the evenings as he prepared dinner or tried to watch the NCAA Final Four games, for example. As the clock wound down, the excitement would mount in the room and so would the acceleration of my fingers on the keyboard.

Eventually my business crept into so many corners of that apartment that we moved into a two-bedroom apartment and set aside the second bedroom for my office. When we moved into a house, I set up office space in a sunny, twelve-by-fourteen-foot back room. I've been there ever since.

I have actually known writers who lived in huge houses and *still* maintained their office space inside their bedrooms. They like it; I think they're nuts. I can't imagine settling back at night to chuckle with Letterman or heckle some wacko on *Nightline*, only to have my fax start cranking out a thirty-page document or a source call me from Australia. The choice is yours—but weigh the consequences of each option.

3. Can you dedicate your at-home work space to your business alone?

While you're thinking about that space dedicated for office use, focus on the word "dedicate." The Internal Revenue Service (IRS) loves that word and wants to make sure that *your* office space is exclusively dedicated to your work only. So, for example, if you have a TV on your desk, make sure your kids don't sit in your office space to watch *Tom & Jerry*. (And, by the way, if you're trying to deduct your TV as an office expense, they can't watch that tube anyway.)

So first figure out where your office space will be, then measure its square footage. If you know your home's total square footage, then you can figure out what percent of your home is dedicated to your work. You will use that calculation to determine what percentage of your heat, your electricity, and so on, you can deduct. But we'll get into those specifics later in this chapter.

4. Is home where the heart and ambition coexist?

Maybe you're just not productive without your personal creature comforts around you. Maybe you dread the idea of working in some foreign space with the same four walls every day. Working at home allows you to customize your workday. Just plug your own variables into a workable equation.

Maybe you like the idea of awakening at 5:30 A.M., putting in two hours in front of the computer, then jogging for an hour and eating breakfast out at the local diner. By 10 A.M., you're back on the computer and work through till 1:30 P.M., when you eat lunch and walk the dogs for a half hour. Starting at 2 P.M., you field phone calls from clients and prospects, until 4 P.M. Then it's time to pick up your sister at the airport, barbecue salmon steaks on the fire escape, and put in a couple more hours on the computer before the late-night news.

All in all, you've had a great day, and you've worked more than nine hours. That's productive. I can't imagine having this kind of flexibility with any other job but mine. And it's possible only because I'm the boss and I keep my office at home.

5. What's your D.Q. (Dedication Quotient)?

If you're going to work at home, you have to measure your level of self-discipline and dedication to your career. Some people are naturally good at avoiding distractions. I'm not. I attach distractions to my life the way other people collect antiques. Maybe it's a problem of perception, but if you crowd your life, as I do sometimes, with non-work-oriented activities, your loved ones will assume your work is an avocation. I constantly fight that battle.

My feeling is that there's no need to punish yourself if you work at home. One of the reasons I and so many other free-lancers work at home is that we enjoy the environment and freedom. Just make sure you avoid the *amoeba syndrome,* as I call it, wherein your hobbies, if not carefully scheduled, just seep and flow into any time slot accessible to them.

Being serious about your work means you'll be concerned about making money from your business, measuring your professional ambitions, and considering how you'd like to shape your business over the next five, ten, and fifteen years. While I like to break up my days into work, recreation, and family chunks, I'm used to biting the bullet when I know that a deadline lies ahead.

6. Do you know how to set "house" rules?

Avoiding and minimizing distractions is one thing. But controlling the human and animal species in your life is quite another thing altogether.

They will take their cue from you. (At least the humans might.) If you're serious and committed to working when you have to, they'll be accustomed to you going into your office, shutting the door, and gluing yourself to the computer. If you're not serious, everyone will think they can traipse in and out of your office, ask you questions, and demand that you do things for them. You, in turn, will do a lot of yelling, to make up for your inconsistent work habits, when you have a major project due on deadline. It can get ugly.

Or you can lay down the law with them and yourself. Sometimes that will mean working when you'd rather be doing something else. But, to quote a family friend: "That's why they call it work."

So how to be taken seriously? Here's a quick checklist of some additional pointers that I'm still incorporating into my own life:

- Make your office off-limits to one and all.
- Hire a babysitter if you're a serious writer-parent.
- Assign yourself specific work and play hours.
- Communicate your schedule to loved ones on a regular basis, to avoid conflicts and prepare everyone when a big project takes over your work life.
- Set up a separate phone line or lines for your office communications and fax/modem.
- Try hard not to answer your home phone during the day.
- Let the answering machine take personal calls. You can check messages on a regular basis. Just don't feel obligated to pick up the phone every time it rings.

Outward Bound

If working at home isn't for you, investigate your options at an office space you might lease or share with another professional. This requires an additional financial commitment from you, but it cures the at-home distraction syndrome. It could also mean a bigger space that's designed for working and comes equipped with all the electronic gadgetry you could need.

The beauty of working in an off-campus locale is that you won't be inclined to procrastinate nearly as much as you would at home. You can leave behind all your personal distractions each day and focus completely on your business. Instead of walking the dogs, paying bills, doing laundry, or organizing the sports closet, you'll only have the computer to stare at. In addition, this might be just the financial commitment that jump-starts your business. After all, the meter will be running.

Consider the following issues when looking for an outside office space for your business:

1. Can you afford a monthly lease that will probably well exceed a typical car payment?

This is a great option, but be ready to cough up some decent cash. A lease will generally require an up-front security deposit of sometimes several months' rent, depending on where you live.

The leasing agent or building owner will put you through financial-approval hoops before agreeing to take you on as a tenant. However, if you live in or near any large city suffering from a depressed commercial real estate market, perhaps some managers will work out a deal if you're willing to commit to a multiyear lease. Negotiations flex considerably in these situations, so you might cut yourself an economical arrangement.

2. Can you afford to have all your work equipment away from home, or can you afford to purchase a second set of equipment for off-hours work?

If you rent an office space, you will bring your computer and all your office supplies to that office away from home. That means you probably won't be able to get substantial amounts of writing done during off-hours. That's OK if you're really productive during the work hours you put in. But, if you live a looser work and life schedule, and can't be that productive, then you have to consider investing in another computer setup at home.

If this presents a financial or work-style hardship, reconsider your choice of leasing a space.

3. Is it possible you'll need office help?

Many professional office buildings offer to bring in office help, equipment, and other on-premises services at their tenants' request. Naturally, this involves some additional costs, but relieves another headache for a writer who would have to contract for these things independently.

The Equipment You Will Need

Free-lancers need to equip their offices with general office supplies, furniture necessities, and personal creature comforts.

You can journey to the neighborhood office supply or stationery store for pens, paper, and a swivel chair, but I recommend doing some shopping. Compare costs once you've determined what exactly you need to make your office a productive, inspiring environment for you.

When I decided I needed a huge, wide, deep desk with a big

open space for my chair, I hunted for a used one, rather than investing some big bucks in a new one. I figured I'd have the best luck at garage sales. Sure enough, I found one at a nearby town's flea market. The seller wanted $100; I snagged it for $50. Not bad.

I bought my executive office chair, file cabinet, and a small credenza for about $125 from a business that advertised a sale of all its furniture when it stopped operating.

My office furniture bears the stamp of thrift-shop utilitarian, but my personal computer, telephones, books, files, and a strategically placed linen runner camouflage the tackier edges. I can live with the ugly, functional stuff as long as I don't violate my key aesthetic and comfort demands: lots of sun and windows, miniblinds, a tile floor, plants, warmly painted walls, and my Chinese screens of flying cranes.

Those may seem like insignificant details, but that's where I invested my office money. You have to decide what environmental elements you need to feel comfortable and then figure out the least-expensive way to furnish the rest of the office.

Computers

All writers need to outfit their offices with some kind of word processing equipment, in order to quickly, efficiently, and accurately crank out copy for clients.

It is quaint for a writer to say he or she still plucks out stories in record time on the old Smith-Corona. However, clients generally do not want hard copy that a secretary must then rekey into the company's word processing units.

As corporations become increasingly automated, they like to know they will receive a compatible computer disk and backup hard copy, or that you can send the copy via computer-based fax or modem directly into their computer system. This simplifies their work life.

Choosing an appropriate, compatible, easy-to-use computer system doesn't have to break your bank. Lately, so many companies manufacture high-quality, high-speed personal computers that there's no need anymore to narrow your choices to a Mac, an IBM, or a clone. It's actually quite mind-boggling to review the available options in your specific price bracket.

If you're a computer virgin, then you need to do some basic research on what personal computers can do for you. Consult the many periodicals at the library that deal exclusively with the personal computing market. These will give you the latest information, reviews, and comparative details about the ever-changing hardware and software options for professionals of every stripe.

Here is a short list of some good personal computing periodicals:

- *Byte*
- *Compute*
- *PC Computing*
- *PC Magazine*
- *PC Week*

Software

You'll also need to research which software will be best for your needs, if you're not familiar with what's out there for basic word processing. When you've narrowed your choices, try them out at a local computer store if at all possible. Many stores have PCs set up and will gladly let you putter around with the applications, as software is sometimes called.

Do not buy software without at least letting someone else demonstrate how it works, since some of the popular word processing applications cost in the $200 to $500 neighborhood. I know now after working on several different kinds that I have preferences about how certain functions should work. They all have idiosyncrasies. You have to know what kinds of questions to ask and what information to look for when choosing a word processing package. Here are some pointers to consider:

Find out how accommodating the software is for a writer.

- Will your writing appear on the screen in the proportions of a sheet of 8.5 × 11 paper when you enter the application?
- Can you access different fonts and layout functions quickly and easily?
- Will you operate in a WYSIWYG (What You See Is What You Get) environment?
- Will you have to learn a lot of codes to navigate through documents?
- Can you arrange documents with larger-type headlines, chapter numbers, subheads, or bullet points easily?

Find out about key functions, such as moving, editing, printing, and deleting text.

- Will the cursor keep up with a writer's speedy fingers?
- How many codes do you have to enter or moves do you have to make to switch around and edit blocks of text?
- How complicated are the print functions?

Find out about the "support" hotline.

- Most software companies operate hotlines for owners. Will it cost you anything to use this service?
- How long are the typical wait times for hotline support?
- How easy is it to read and understand the documentation supplied with the system?

Find out about application upgrades.

- How will those upgrades affect your existing hardware and operating system?
- How much memory and power will your system need to optimally run the upgraded software?
- How often does the software company put out upgrades?
- How difficult will it be for you to do the upgrade yourself?

If you read some of the personal computing magazines out there, you'll find exhaustive product reviews and analyses of support quality. This can be quite an issue if you're working on a document, can't figure how to make some function work, and then spend a half hour trying to get through to the manufacturer's hotline. Many product reviews routinely cover these areas, but will be invisible to you, the purchaser, when you look over software boxes in a store.

Get the Right Fit

Probably the next most important issue facing you as you choose your personal computer hardware and word processing software is to find out what clients use and what will interface well with their systems.

You can't please everybody, but you should be able to accommodate your clients' needs if your software package has an easy-to-use *conversion* system. That will allow you to take a document from your computer, copy it to a disk, and translate it into the computer language (software) that your client's computers can read.

Modems and Faxes

Sending documents by modem and fax is becoming as simple and inexpensive as a typical phone call. That's because you don't have to buy those big old fax machines or funny phone-modem cradles anymore, if you outfit your personal computer with a fax/modem application.

These programs are inexpensive alternatives that allow you to transmit documents straight from your computer to anyone who needs them, as long as the recipient has the appropriate hardware and software. Some of my clients' information systems are so up-to-speed that I don't have to give them my finished product as hard copy or on a computer disk anymore. I merely transmit the document through the phone lines directly from my computer. I never have to touch any hard copy. This greatly reduces my overnight mail and local messenger costs, and simplifies my personal and collaborative editing.

On the other hand, I also like having my fax machine available in case I hand-edit existing hard copy, which I must then send back to a client. But that is a rarity.

Laptops and Notebooks

Writers often find themselves inspired at odd moments. It's then that they wish they had a laptop or notebook computer handy.

Unfortunately, these skinny, magical, personal computers in slim briefcases tote hefty price tags. They're a luxury for the typical free-lancer, who probably is investing heavily in a decent tabletop system and its continuous upgrades. However, I know a couple writers who skipped the at-home fixed system completely and committed themselves to a high-end notebook computer.

You can outfit such a computer with all the power, software, and speed of a desktop system, but you'll pay for it.

Tax Considerations

When you commit to becoming a free-lance writer, you have to consider how this probably will change your tax status. This book isn't meant as the final word in self-employment tax advice, by any stretch of the most acrobatic imagination. Consult a qualified accountant for the most appropriate advice for your situation, and see Appendix III for a list of useful tax guides. However, there are some basics you need to know from the very beginning of your business.

As a self-employed person, you will no longer have some employer withholding income from your paychecks for federal, state, social security, and unemployment compensation taxes. You have to do all this yourself now, or suffer the legal consequences of not reporting income to the government. Dodging tax obligations is not a terrific idea for someone trying to establish a business and a long-term reputation.

You're the boss, which is great. But that also brings with it the responsibility to report all your income from your business and then pay the correct amount of tax on that income.

1. Self-Employed Estimated Tax Payments

Sole proprietors don't have any income withheld from checks, and the IRS requests that you make quarterly payments based on a projected income level for the coming year. The IRS financially penalizes self-employed workers who postpone these payments until April 15 and send in a lump-sum payment for the year. Again, consult a qualified accountant for some advice about your situation.

You will probably operate your business as a *sole proprietorship* and not as a *corporation*. That means you work by yourself, for yourself, and don't have to fill out a lot of the paperwork that you do if you incorporate your business. Incorporating your business is a good idea, however, if you have other people coming to your home office, either to work for you or to visit as clients. If they are injured while they are in your home, your business can legally take the financial blows—instead of you personally.

Naturally you should find out if there are any legal requirements or restrictions—zoning and licensing—for setting up a business as a sole proprietor in your town. If not, all you need for tax reporting anything about your business is your social security number and a Schedule C, which enumerates your business income and expenses.

2. Delicious Deductions

Some or all the costs of many items and services can probably be deducted from your taxes, as long as they're all related to your business, you save all your receipts, and you keep a close record of all your expenses. An accountant can give you the latest information and the most appropriate advice for your particular situation.

Some of these expenses might include a computer, paper, pencils, pens, desks, calendars, telephones, tape recorders, files, folders, and portfolios. You will also pay for gas to drive to your clients' offices and other destinations in order to complete assignments. You may pay for client lunches, skill-building seminars, and business trips. Then there are the expenses related to maintaining your actual home office, including utilities, maid service, carpet cleaning (if it's in your office), window cleaning, and so on. You can probably deduct a percentage of these expenses equal to the percentage of your home that is dedicated to your office and work.

To calculate what percentage of your home is used exclusively for your office, you might want to refer to an actual blueprint or drawn layout of your house, with all its square footage indicated. Such a document would go a long way toward convincing an IRS agent that you seriously conduct business in your house. And stick to a hard-and-fast rule of keeping it exclusively for work alone. Never lie to cover up for nonprofessional use of the space.

3. Keeping Records

Keep accurate and detailed records of all money that flows in and out of your business. Compulsive bookkeeping will keep you from having to store every detail of your business life in your head, and will help keep the IRS wolves at bay.

Many people opt to record all their expenses and income on their personal computer. That's a great option if your computer can accommodate the additional software. The simplest systems can be equally effective, even if all you do is write your income in a ledger each time you receive a check and save all your receipts in a handy-dandy accordion file.

Just choose a system and stick with it for at least a year. After that, you can change it. In my experience, changing midstream can mess up your accounting.

Ideally, after you buy a business-related item or service, write down on the receipt what that thing was purchased for and to what part of your business it is related. Sometimes you'll need to write dates on receipts, because the date already on the receipt may be wrong, illegible, or missing. Then you'll write down the expense in a specific category in your ledger.

If you're a really dutiful little sole proprietor, you'll save each week's worth of receipts and write them down according to how the IRS breaks down the Schedule C expense categories. Then you won't be pulling out your hair next April as you try to figure out what you spent your money on and how you should account for all of it.

One long-term piece of tax-planning advice I try to follow if I'm having a great year is to cram as many expenses into the end of the year as possible. I also try to postpone some December invoicing so I don't receive my checks until the next January. This is legal and smart. Just be sure you never falsify information concerning when you were actually paid or when you actually cashed a check.

4. Your Car (or Other Transportation)

If you drive your car for work, you will be able to deduct a generous portion of your car's expenses from your gross income: insurance, monthly payments, maintenance, gas, and so on. Either that or you will track all your car mileage for work (which you should do anyway) and then deduct a certain amount per mile.

Whichever approach you take with your car expenses, I recommend consulting an accountant for the latest information and appropriate advice for your particular situation. There are many nuances to car deductions that you can explore.

You also need to decide whether to lease or buy that car for work. Leasing is cheaper, generally, than buying the same car. And if you can keep your mileage under a specific annual amount (say, twelve thousand or fifteen thousand miles), you can negotiate a nifty lease payment. Then, after four years, for example, you bring back the car and start over again.

Read the fine print in lease deals you see in the newspaper. Oftentimes they minimize your up-front obligation, which could be a down payment, a trade-in, or a couple of monthly payments.

5. Entertainment and Travel

Any time you pay for a client's meals and conduct some business simultaneously, you can deduct at least a portion of the costs: food, parking, tips, cabs, and so on. Once again, just save the receipts and write down what you talked about and who lunched with you. Make sure the dates and prices are clearly marked on your receipt.

If you travel for business, often clients will pay for your expenses. If not, definitely save the receipts and deduct these costs. When you travel somewhere for work-related seminars, conventions, or other events, you can write off most of your expenses. Just save receipts and check any marginally acceptable expenses with your accountant. For instance, the IRS might look askance if you try to deduct a massage, a movie in your hotel room, or similar incidentals. Again, see Appendix III for a list of useful tax guides.

6. Medical Insurance

Free-lancers are sole proprietors—self-employed people without any company sharing medical insurance responsibilities. Don't hold out for a federally subsidized health insurance plan; you owe it to yourself to have some kind of coverage, even if it's only a last-ditch, big-deductible, catastrophic plan. The IRS lets you deduct some or all of many medical costs you pay out-of-pocket, over and above an insurance premium. Once again, consult a tax expert on these matters.

Just remember that few people can afford the astronomical costs of a hospital stay. Unless you're Ivana Trump or similarly bankrolled, you should avoid living without any health insurance coverage. One visit to the emergency room, with a few X rays, blood tests, some stitches, some bandages, examination by a specialist, intravenous hookups, and any medications, can easily run up a hospital tab in the thousands.

If you don't want to bankrupt your family's personal finances, you better consider buying some coverage. Or, if it is an option for you, see if you can be added to your mate's policy. Consult any of the associations listed in Chapter XII, "The Networking Necessity," for more information on their group insurance plans.

With a firm handle on the financial, computing, and office-space needs of your free-lance business, you'll be ready to focus on what work actually exists out there for you.

Chapter IV

Learn the Nuts and Bolts of Corporate Writing

CORPORATE DEPARTMENTS that dish out free-lance communications assignments might fall under different titles: Public Relations, Corporate Communications, Promotions, Public Affairs, Media Relations, or possibly Training. Whatever the department or heading used, the assignments can all be classified as either internal or external communications, depending on the audience. (Look for more information about sniffing out specific sources in Chapter VI, "Navigate the Marketing Maze.")

Internal corporate communicators might call on free-lancers for any or all of the following:

- Newsletters for internal/external audiences
- Marketing magazine articles
- Brochures
- Meeting and presentation materials
- Press releases
- Audio/visual scripts
- Interactive computer programs integrating several media
- Speeches
- Annual financial reports
- Employee annual reports
- Letters from top executives
- Trade press ghostwritten articles
- Copywriting or advertising writing

- Technical writing
- Big project coordination

I explain these in detail later in this chapter.

The Target Audience

A company's possible audiences for these internally produced communications might include employees, managers, stockholders, the surrounding community, customers, the trade, or consumers. The internal communicator identifies the informational needs of those audiences and tailors the company's publications or communiqués accordingly. Your first job, therefore, is to understand the target audience.

The more recent trend toward greater corporate candor in disseminating information to a corporation's various audiences has led to spicier, more meaningful communications. Historically, these communications covered such mundane subjects as the corporate baseball team scores, product announcements, marketing campaign explanations, and semicanned commentaries from high executives.

Now a company might be just as likely to produce articles, brochures, interactive computer disks, or videos that:

- Show employees how to finance their children's college education
- Explain to managers how to help an employee who's in a substance abuse recovery program
- Describe to the surrounding community how the company's disaster recovery program works and affects everyone
- Present the company's efforts to upgrade its pollution-control operations

So what is it all these people—audiences—want and need to know about any given company? Probably the company's financial health will concern them most. Then they'll want to know how they personally will be affected by the company's financial fluctuations and any changes to the company's product lines and services. But employees, often attuned to their tenuous future at their company, want to understand and be privy to all the company's actions.

With a greater awareness of the world's fragile environment, companies find themselves held accountable to a far greater audience than ever. Steven Ross, associate professor of Professional Practice at Columbia University's Graduate School of Journalism, concurs that it is imperative these days for a company to explain its position on these matters and describe the steps it is taking to be a conscientious corporate neighbor.

"There are more demands on companies to be responsive to a wider audience," says Ross. "It used to be that if a reporter would walk up and say the place smelled bad, they'd tell us to go away. Now they're publishing reports and responding to our inquiries more vigilantly. They're more aware of the consequences of not communicating."

In addition, with political and economic barriers dropping worldwide, a more global marketplace is evolving. To keep up with and capitalize on new opportunities, companies find themselves dealing with different customers, different cultures, new risks.

Understanding all the variables that possibly influence a company's financial health is particularly key for those who have a stake in the company—employees, managers, stockholders, and customers. So why do all these groups need to be included in the information continuum?

- *Employees*—so they feel included and understand why it is they are doing what they're doing
- *Managers*—so they can explain everything to employees and keep open communication channels
- *Stockholders*—so they know how their investments are being

used; and that they're being used wisely and for everyone's greater profit

- *Customers*—so they can see if company actions are being taken with their wants and needs in mind

This increasing circle of influence, accountability, and responsibility causes companies to produce information positioned in a wider context. What are the long-term objectives and ramifications of the recent plant expansion? Why is managed health care something employees should learn more about? What are the benefits of the plant's investing in new pollution-effluent controls? Why should employees know more about business customs in Indonesia?

Free-lancers must understand that companies increasingly communicate information with this wider global, economic, legal, and political context in mind. And as the subject areas continue to broaden, the range of communications options widens and changes to keep pace. Progressive communicators regularly experiment with new technologies and adapt conventional devices to give their messages more pizzazz, appeal, and effectiveness. Once you know your target audience, you will be better able to reach them through the different communications options.

What Corporations Buy

An all-purpose free-lance writer, also known as a communications generalist, will want to perfect his or her writing and handling of many different communications forms. Although I consider myself a generalist, newsletter articles, marketing magazine pieces, brochures, and script-writing form the guts of my business. These are mainstay, flexible communication vehicles for most companies and often turn out to be a writer's niche with different clients. This translates into repeat business.

• **Newsletters** are common corporate communications devices that can turn into long-term, lucrative gigs for free-lancers. The newsletter format is common to many companies because of its flexibility. It can mold to different workplaces, budgets, artistic situations, and potential subjects to be covered. Even the smallest of companies typically produces some kind of bulletin or newspaper for employees.

It is important to in-house personnel that they do not have to find someone new to write for each issue of a regularly published newsletter. In-house corporate communications people hire free-lancers for these assignments because they want the work done efficiently, economically, and painlessly. They should be able to assume that a clear-writing, self-starting outside contractor will get that publication out on time, and will be devoted to doing so.

The client also wants consistency of writing and minimal personnel hassles, otherwise why not have a full-time employee handle the newsletter and more? The most logical rationale for not doing so is that a free-lancer is more economical. The company avoids paying a full-timer's salary, overhead, office space, expenses, insurance benefits, and additional compensations.

Companies produce newsletters in a myriad of formats. I've worked on publications varying from weekly black-and-white single-pagers off the copier to a forty-page, four-color weekly tabloid that rivals *USA Today* in story volume and range of topics covered. At different companies, the newsletter may serve different audiences and purposes. Generally, the more strategic, comprehensive, and inclusive the publication, the more important it is to the company. Get yourself hooked into these kinds of vital publications if you can.

Publications that don't have any strategic value or purpose within an organization are often short-lived and among the first bits of chaff cut from the wheat when a company implements cost-effectiveness programs. When you look at a publication to measure its quality and apparent value to the company, scrutinize whether it fulfills any of the following objectives:

- Informs employees of company events
- Enumerates personnel changes, promotions, and openings
- Reports company sporting events/accomplishments
- Draws employees into the corporate "family" by quoting rank and file
- Serves as a marketing tool as well
- Makes customers/competition aware of internal doings
- Outlines long-term corporate strategy for employees
- Applauds employees' contributions to corporate success
- Beefs up morale by its tone and approach

While a prospective or existing client may not apprise you of these specific objectives, it won't be difficult to discern those goals and whether the writing accomplishes the task. Look for articles that discuss all different parts of the company, its strategies, and its people, such as:

- Strikingly candid Q&A with the CEO about a new productivity concept
- A profile of a production line worker who simplified some process
- A tip list for dealing with customers around the world
- Results from an employee survey about job satisfaction
- Feature about a new-product team that integrated employees from all areas
- A discussion of why the company is closing an office
- The rationale for a new employee contribution to health-care costs, accompanied by "man-on-the-street" comments from employees
- Hints for working parents on how to simplify life
- A tip list for employees facing outplacement or early retirement

Additionally, if you want to really psychoanalyze a publication and its strategic value, study its many content, attitude, writing style, and design dimensions. This will help you adapt to the newsletter's style, choose the most appropriate samples to show a potential client, and eventually pitch story topics to the client.

• The **marketing magazine** format takes the company newsletter to new heights of sophistication and wider audience potential. OK, it costs more to produce—lots more. But, boy, when a company distributes a slick quarterly publication with writing that is as hot as its design, everyone's impressed.

Ideally, employees and retirees bust their buttons with pride that they're part of such a high-quality organization, customers surmise that they're dealing with a high-profile company when they witness the care put into the publication, stockholders want a bigger piece of the pie, and the trade feels its competitive pulse racing to keep up.

Generally only blue-chip companies produce these big-ticket publications. It's just not worth it for a small, less-endowed company to invest in such a publication. A quality production requires top writing, which sometimes means contracting articles from name authors with specific industry expertise. Then, the company can marquee the author's name on the publication cover.

The price tag for such publications' design, layout, and writing can run equal to a semester at a top-ranking private university. And, of course, the paper stock should be classy, high-quality stuff of some significant weight.

All in all, these mouthpiece publications are meant to impress and attract readers to turn the pages because of their visual appeal, slick writing, provocative coverage, and celebrity authorship. A free-lancer needs to understand the significant investment these companies make in such a publication, in order to gauge his or her own possible role in the publication, to discuss most diplomatically the magazine's qualities (in positive terms always), and to offer constructive ideas for the magazine's future.

- **Brochures** stand as a tried-and-true method for disseminating specific information to a wide audience. When companies invent new products or services (or change old ones), they might announce the news to the media via press releases, then follow up with brochures for customers and the trade. These brochures often include more nuts and bolts about the product/service couched in jazzier language than is fit for a traditional press release.

Most companies also produce "identity" brochures of some sort that describe the company's origins, philosophies, products, and services. In addition, they may print infomercial and public relations brochures directed at consumers who may not be aware of some community service project or indirect benefit they're receiving from a company product or service.

Public service brochures can genuinely benefit consumers if they accurately inform them about some subject. These publications can communicate the company's stance on a political issue, elaborate on some related hot-button social issue, solicit the public for additional support in a given area, or clarify the company's actions on a possibly negative situation. Generally these brochures are more common among big companies, which have the money to invest in such high-profile communications projects.

Brochure-writing opportunities abound at bigger companies and come in all different shapes and sizes. For instance, I'm called in regularly to write longer **pamphlets** or **booklets** on different subjects pertinent to clients. These communicate more in-depth information about specific topics than might be already covered in smaller four-, eight-, or twelve-page brochures. I find that my article-writing and brochure-writing skills merge well in the longer assignments. When I pitch for such assignments, I play up the complementary nature of my versatile writing skills.

- Internal communicators often assign a free-lancer to write the copy for **meeting and presentation materials** when the in-house staff is swamped dealing with all the details of the meeting itself.

This package assignment might include writing:

- The advance informational brochure for the meeting-goers
- A newsletter article
- Talking points for panel speakers
- Formal pass-around outlines for discussion topics
- A follow-up special edition newsletter focused on the meeting events
- Lists of provocative, brain-teasing concepts for informal roundtable brainstorm sessions
- Speeches for headline speakers

You might be called on to write any one or all of these items, depending on how crunched the internal staffers feel.

- Many big companies rely on **press releases** to communicate to the media about new actions, staff appointments, products, or services. These communications pieces are usually brief and conventionally formatted, and adopt a serious, hard-news approach for credibility's sake. They are sent by the usual mail services, by fax, or via different computer linkup services.

Internal people generally have the information at their fingertips and can write press releases in half the time it would take to explain the subject to a free-lancer. This is particularly true in the case of a sudden event that has provoked immediate attention by the press, compressing the communicator's time frame. The press releases I usually write as a free-lancer are part of big, long-term projects that offer the luxury of advance planning and significant lead time.

- Many companies produce a lot of **videos, slide shows,** and **multimedia presentations** to disseminate specific information to a narrow audience. Used for training, step-by-step instructionals, product launches, and major public relations campaigns, these communications pieces require a writer to work in a different format and with a different approach from brochure copywriting or news/feature writing.

Scripts for audio assignments only ask the writer to blend together narrative, sound-bite quotes, and/or sound effects. Scripts for video assignments are quite a bit more complicated. They require the writer to skillfully coordinate these items with the gamut of possible visual elements as well as a column format. Any writer who delves into script writing needs to learn the basics of video production and editing before attempting these assignments. It also helps to have a sharp eye for what looks good on camera. (Look for more information on this in Chapter X, "Free-Lance Writer as Art Director.")

• Some companies now opt to produce the same kinds of training and informational communications on **interactive computer disks.** These media are becoming more common, with networked personal computers, software that integrates sound and image, and high-definition color monitors. In five to ten years, they'll probably be ubiquitous.

I've helped some clients produce these disk programs for a variety of purposes:

• To explain complex product information to customers
• To help employees sign up for benefits
• To help trade show attendees learn the features of products/ services
• To communicate an individual department's services and potential to a corporate-wide audience
• To orient new employees to company programs and benefits

Most companies aren't even aware how well this medium works to get across messages. It can convey far more information in a lively format than can a printed brochure. Users can learn the information in private, at their own speed, and pick and choose which sections they want to explore, via a menu format.

Producing these disk programs can be quite costly, and the technology is still somewhat raw, so not too many companies opt to communicate to many audiences this way. The ones that do commit to turning out these twenty-first-century communications devices better be ready to invest big bucks in the software's design in particular. Most such software has to be customized, but some can be built on templated programs that software engineers design, lease as is, or customize for a particular client's needs.

Once a company fine-tunes the software, making diskette copies is the least expensive part of the project.

Fortunately for writers, the scripts differ only slightly from typical audiovisual scripts. It pays to coordinate up front with the software designer, to understand how much of the writing can be devoted to voice and sound versus on-screen narratives and images. Every on-screen element and every sound bite or effect eats up memory on a disk.

Find out the limits of the eventual disk or personal computer network and work from there. This may mean you have to settle for a lot more narrative that is scrolled, dissolved, or popped onto the screen as a visual image. It doesn't require as much memory as graphic images or sound.

• **Speeches** are a backbone communications device for most companies. Although some big companies have on-staff, specialized speech writers to crank these out for executives and managers, crunch times do occur and free-lancers might get the nod.

Corporate executives or managers rarely speak off the cuff. Few reasons would compel them to risk revealing incorrect information, speaking inarticulately or without an organized approach. A well-written, rehearsed speech takes a load off any corporate speaker—in any situation.

Writing these pieces as a free-lancer means receiving the assignment from an internal person, and then usually sitting down with the speaker for a topical interview or discussion. This gives the writer the chance to listen to the speaker's typical vocabulary, vocal mannerisms, speaking rhythm, and anxiety regarding the upcoming speech. I like to tape these interviews, with the speaker's permission, to ensure that my memory doesn't fail me when recalling the subject areas to be covered as well as the speaker's idiosyncrasies.

Take your cue from the speaker as far as organization, the word flow and style you use in the speech. That helps minimize the rewrites and dissatisfaction. You don't want to hear these words: "I don't talk like that."

• Although practically all companies (big and small, public and private) produce some sort of **annual financial report,** they may not produce them for everyone's eyes. Companies that sell shares of stock on any exchange are public and are required to produce a comprehensive financial report every year. These reports break down the company's financial status by the fiscal quarter and compare its results over several previous years.

Companies that publish these reports for the public often produce them in a slick, colorful format that incorporates a significant amount of warm and fuzzy narrative about the company's products/services and performance high points. This calls for some equally slick writing that seamlessly integrates a discussion of financial matters with company braggadocio. While some companies staff individuals who specialize in writing the annual report, others might call on free-lancers, or opt for a consulting agency that specializes in this kind of writing.

Because stockholders are not all necessarily finance wizards, it's important to write the information conversationally and explain technical material in clear laypeople's terms. It's not an easy job to sift through volumes of spreadsheet data listing revenues, capitalization investments, long-term liabilities, and other dollar figures, and then describe fluidly how and why the company performed the way it did. And, to top it off, you have to try to make the company sound productive, savvy, progressive, and smart (if not profitable), regardless of what its actual financial status may be.

Free-lancers who luck into these regularly scheduled writing slots may find they need only consolidate and fine-tune some company person's financial analyses. The real challenge, again, is to put some positive spin on what many times is mixed news. Many companies rely on the same annual report writers for years and pay them munificently for their services.

• **Employee annual reports** are often published simultaneously with annual financial reports. Many big companies recognize that the annual report may not be every employee's preferred reading material, except perhaps at bedtime. But the financial status of the company may still be top of mind for many employees—given the euphemistic "rightsizing" trends at so many companies. So some kind of employee annual report might be the way to explain the company's status in terms of how employees contributed to the company's success and how they adapted to company changes and challenges.

These communications pieces are often as slickly presented as the official annual report and might be distributed to shareholders and others outside the employee base. There is no single, successful formula for these reports. However, the format might serve up a string of brief profiles of outstanding employee dedication, contribution, and courage, backed up with the individuals' photos.

Additionally, the editor might include a year-in-review introduction and a couple of articles highlighting the year's ups and downs and how employees measured up. Throughout these narrations, the editor might blend in germane financial news.

Free-lancers called on to write these so-called employee annual reports could be asked to contribute one or more articles to such a publication. The style tends to be a feature-story approach, with even more heartwarming language positioned in a slick copy layout.

• Corporate executives and managers sometimes call on communications departments to help them produce **letters** to employees, stockholders, or the trade. Usually brief in length, these may be as simple as an announcement about a new benefits program, a retirement good-bye, or a major staff appointment.

They can also discuss more heady topics, such as how the company plans to face a specific political, environmental, or personnel problem. In any case, writing these letters is a fairly straightforward proposition, as they are typically styled in serious but accessible language in one page.

• A derivative communications assignment is to **ghostwrite** or **edit trade press articles** for corporate executives. Free-lancers who develop a knack for writing accurate, entertaining articles for a corporation may find themselves asked to edit or ghostwrite articles for those company's executives who have been asked to write something for an industrial or other outside publication.

More often than not, the executive has a dramatic business story to convey and can't make it come alive on paper. Typically, he or she sweats through the writing and organizational process, but the article reads like the telephone book. So the executive taps a professional writer for fine-tuning.

I have often been able to give these executives a lift by telling them all the information is there, "we" just need to tighten up the writing and cut down the fatty language interfering with the message. So although these assignments sometimes start out as writing jobs, they can transform themselves into mere editing exercises.

• Occasionally a free-lance corporate writing assignment may resemble a **copywriting** or **technical writing job**. Generally, however, the bigger the company, the more segregated these two areas are from a company's internal/external communications functions. The type of writing required is quite a departure from the typical assignments faced by a free-lance corporate communicator, unless that communicator regularly cranks out consumer/trade ad copy for a given company.

Copywriting jobs for print and audiovisual advertisements might be aimed at some overlapping audiences for a company's regular communications, but they are often coordinated, farmed out, and managed differently. Many corporations have sales promotion, marketing, or advertising staffers who work as liaisons with outside advertising agencies to manage a product's total trade/consumer advertising presence. The bigger the company, the more likely it is that these responsibilities will be dealt with by individual product staffs and possibly even different ad agencies.

This can be a lucrative side of the free-lance writing world, if a writer is willing to pursue a different marketing path than the one I recommend for landing corporate communications projects. Several good books can guide writers through this different process.

• Although some internal/external communications assignments might require a free-lancer to understand or incorporate technical information into a piece, I wouldn't qualify this as **technical writing** per se.

I define technical writing assignments as instruction manuals, installation pamphlets, training guides, operator instructions, and other straight, factual written materials needed for companies that engineer, produce, or provide complex products/services to various industries and consumers.

Some technical writers work full-time for an individual company, while others work free-lance or contract with a technical agency or broker that farms out the writer's services to client-companies. Oftentimes the writing is produced by the engineers who actually designed the products.

Technical writing itself tends to be academic, instructional, and serious. Understandably, a company that produces radial arm saws, for instance, doesn't want an instruction manual's zingy copy to obscure key factual information.

On the other hand, more companies should let free-lance corporate communications writers take a shot at writing technical copy. Maybe then assembling a bicycle, installing software, or retiling a bathroom would be easier (and safer) and the non-gearheads of the world would be kept from contributing to the "expletives deleted" lexicon.

We generalist corporate writers frequently jump into assignments with a smattering of knowledge about the subject. Then we proceed to synthesize stacks of information and figure out the best way to explain it to someone just like ourselves. So if you feel adept at converting complex information into laypeople's terms, then don't be afraid to bill yourself as a technical writer. Even if you know little about a subject, you might end up being the perfect translator for a target audience.

• You really step up your income potential when a corporation hitches its wagon to your star for a **major project**. Perhaps you've inspired confidence by your ability to produce clean, accurate, lively copy on deadline. Then the client brings you in as part of a bigger team tackling a major corporate endeavor.

Sometimes these all-hands-on-deck projects are promotional campaigns for a new product, service, or corporate effort. The projects may be multifaceted, multimedia blitzes for any of the corporation's internal or external audiences.

For example, one client launched a quality program and wanted to spread the word about its three-year company effort.

First, the client brought in a team of quality consultants to audit the company's quality status and employee awareness of that quality. Armed with the consultants' findings, an internal team continued the project. The communications people coordinated with the quality team to structure an appropriate plan.

The combined team identified several communications devices to disseminate the program's specifics to employees, announce the company's undertaking to the media, and to train managers in heading up the interdepartmental quality teams. These internal teams' mission was to scrutinize every angle of the company's workings from the perspective that every employee counts, everyone has customers, and everyone needs to understand and adjust to his or her customers' needs and wants.

Two different newsletters emerged to keep the information exchange flowing on two different levels: the microcosmic, individual quality accomplishments witnessed throughout the company; and the big-picture strategy of the entire program as it evolved. The company also worked closely with the local and trade press to explain the program and to position articles that featured the company's efforts. While all this was going on, the communications team, including me, coordinated several other communications efforts:

- An overall look and enduring theme for most print and visual materials
- A brochure to explain the program to customers and the trade
- A training video explaining the different stages of the program
- A portable photo display featuring employees' experiences with the campaign
- An incentive effort with prizes to entice employees to come up with new ways to beef up quality
- Employee brown-bag lunches to announce results of the incentive program and new teams' accomplishments

Free-lancers who are involved in such a project may end up writing all the copy for the project or just a piece of the pie. Regardless, you are a member of the team and valued as such.

Sometimes an overarching theme has already been devised by management and an ad agency, perhaps before the writer comes on board to take over different written parts of the project. In that case, the writer will be asked to blend in or work around a given slogan, logo, or concept. The assembled team tackling these big communications projects may come from inside or outside the company and might include any of the following staffers:

- Advertising agency representatives
- Graphics/design firm people

- Audio/visual specialists
- Internal communications liaisons
- Corporate operations people
- Administrative representatives
- Product-service specialists
- Legal consultants
- Top management

Several group strategy meetings may be planned to devise an overall concept to ensure consistency throughout the campaign's parts and cohesion among the team members. Once the team cements the theme, look, and tone for the blitz, then the individual members go off on their own to fulfill their specialized responsibilities. Typically, some central person will serve as coordinator for the whole project and keep team members informed of the project's progress and completion target dates.

"The team, the team, the team."

In those words, Bo Schembechler, the former University of Michigan football coach, summarized the need to appreciate and work within the confines and synergism of "the team." The same applies to free-lance writers working with a team composed of disparate corporate staffers on a communications project. Because free-lancers are used to working solo, it can be startling for them to be thrust into a team situation.

Your collaborative skills may need a wake-up call. This means you need to listen more, talk less, take lots of notes at meetings, and consult other team members not just for expertise but for feedback on your own ideas. Consider the merits of all brainstormed ideas offered for your piece of the job.

Your ability to adapt to the group's dynamics in meetings and on conference calls can help you become a key member of the team. Otherwise, the label of "arrogant maverick" might glue itself to you. It is possible to blend in without subordinating your creative input or personality. But remember, the group and its objectives are more important than any of the individuals alone.

Relish the free-flowing wealth of an uninhibited creative group; show your versatility.

And remember, these big projects might offer you new opportunities to network and market your skills to other potential clients, inside and outside the specific corporate circle.

Are You a Generalist or Specialist?

In addition to learning about the types of assignments out there, you need to analyze whether or not you might target your writing services at a specific industry. Sit down and dissect the potential benefits and downfalls of narrowing your market focus and becoming an expert rather than a generalist writer.

Before you begin, look at your past experience and determine if specializing could be your ace. (Check out Chapter I, "The Successful Start-Up," for more information on analyzing your free-lance aptitude.) I've known writers who did this and now command between $125 and $150 per hour for their writing services. They're in demand, often because the industries they write about are complex and/or high-tech.

Although there are hundreds of industries and companies in which you can carve your free-lance niche, you need to know the assets and weaknesses you would bring to each type of client. While reviewing the following charts, think objectively about how you fit into each of the categories and how comfortable you are within those kinds of environments.

A well-defined niche will bring out the best in you, but you must sort out and focus your talents to determine your most appropriate path.

After you've fine-tuned a corporate writing profile, the next chapter will help you determine which companies to approach.

The advantages of focusing on a specific industry	The disadvantages of focusing on a specific industry
You earn the reputation as a hot, knowledgeable industry resource.	If your portfolio and samples aren't quite up to par, it's hard to prove your credibility.
Your expertise is your marketing leverage.	You might not be able to invest the time it takes to track down all the businesses in that one industry.
You become an expert source for consumer and trade press articles.	Traveling is an integral part of the job.
Trade groups and meeting organizers may feature you as a panel "expert."	You can't focus on a region; you must focus globally.
You attract technical writing agencies that can send you regular business.	You need to latch onto an industry that is growing, thriving, and fairly impervious to market fluctuations.
Your market is everywhere the industry may be.	You might need outside help to identify new markets, which would mean spending time selling yourself to technical-writing agencies.
Clients will pay for your byline on most any print piece.	

The advantages of being a generalist

Keeps your writing business recession-proof.

Enables you to try your hand at different types of writing and industries.

Introduces you to people in different professions.

Places you in different corporate environments.

Teaches you about many industries, product lines, and services.

May not require excessive traveling.

Allows you to market your many writing abilities and versatility.

You can focus on a region if you want.

The disadvantages of being a generalist

Clients aren't really sure what you're good at.

Stamps you with stigma of dilettantism.

You never entrench yourself in one industry.

You constantly need to upgrade your portfolio and juggle samples around.

You are competing for assignments with many more available free-lancers.

Pay potential is not as high, unless you're well established and sought after by clients.

You never feel you're building a solid knowledge base about anything in particular.

You have a tough time defining your strengths and weaknesses.

Chapter V

Find Your Corporate Niche

JUST AS YOU HAVE targeted the types of corporate writing opportunities out there, you should also determine what type of company you'll click with best. Like the animal kingdom, companies come in all different sizes, shapes, and personalities. You'll find yourself choosing among ones that exhibit different characteristics on many levels: large or small; single industry or conglomerate; regional or global orientation; service provider, product manufacturer, or both; territorial carnivore or gentle herbivore.

Begin by considering the pros and cons of each category (or combination of categories) and see where you might best market your talents. Ask yourself these questions:

- What type of environment makes you most comfortable?
- Do you shudder at the thought of knocking on the door of some Fortune 500 company?
- Would you feel more at ease working with people who don't wear suits?
- Do you like to travel?
- Would you like to have more control over a project's total coordination?
- What type of industry do you find appealing, accessible, and understandable?
- Are you opposed to working for a company that produces toxic chemicals?
- Have you had financial writing experience, and do you want to investigate writing only for insurance carriers and banks?

As your writing career progresses, you will gain more perspective on how you've either expanded your markets or specialized in a certain area. Monitoring your growth can help you decide how to expand your business and make smooth segues from one category of corporate communications to another. You may find more overlap in the markets you've successfully conquered than you think.

Size Counts

Large and small companies both have advantages and disadvantages for the free-lance writer trying to solicit business. A Fortune 500 company and the fifteen-person construction contractor in the next town have different needs, expectations, budgets, and restrictions.

However, every business that hires you has the same goal: to communicate with its key audiences as identified in Chapter IV, "Learn the Nuts and Bolts of Corporate Writing." You have to determine which corporate size and type appeals to you more, since the size of a company will affect your dynamics within that company, and each of them offers different challenges when you're marketing yourself.

Use the following charts to help you weigh how the advantages and disadvantages of large and small corporations will affect you.

I've drawn up these lists based on my own experience with many different companies. Granted, not every company you'll work with will reflect all (or possibly any) of the characteristics I have included. And you'll probably see some overlapping qualities between small and large companies.

One way or the other, monitor the large and small companies with whom you do business. You'll begin to see profiles shaping up and some contrasting approaches in how they conduct their communications operations. If you have trouble working within the confines of those qualities, then you'll know which type of prospects to avoid in the future.

Only this kind of understanding can solidify the target list of prospective clients that you'll develop.

Make Your List, Check It Thrice!

Once you've analyzed your background strengths and weaknesses, and then mulled over what size of company or specific industry appeals to you most, you can create a target list of prospective corporate clients. While it's a bit more cumbersome and painstaking at the beginning, your target list (and your business) should practically start to generate itself as your business grows. My personal experience has been that once I had a foothold at one company, I was able to parlay that experience into new business at another company.

You've drawn up your ideal company profile, and you've probably collected some names of specific companies you've read or heard about. Now it's time to dig up information on those companies, by putting in serious library time. You need to have at your fingertips as much knowledge about your top choices as possible.

This information will:

- Impress prospective clients because it shows you know something about the company. You don't want to sit mutely as a corporate communicator runs through a series of product acronyms that you easily could have learned by reading a company publication or even the annual report.
- Help you avoid asking too many simple questions that reveal your basic ignorance about the company.

- Give you something to talk about during awkward prospect meetings and phone conversations. When you don't know anything about the company, you sound dumb. The lack of shared knowledge can stymie conversation.
- Give you an idea up front of how deep a prospective client's pockets are and whether the client is in a financial position to be launching more communications projects. By reading any recent articles about the company, you'll know better what its status is and whether communications have plunged off the priority list.
- Offer insight into the company's communications attitude.

Possible advantages of a large corporate client	Possible disadvantages of a large corporate client
Sophisticated communications department	Less creative latitude; prescriptive writing
Sophisticated in-house production facility	Pigeonholed writers
Liberal use of outside designers/photographers	A complex management structure to navigate when marketing yourself
Corporate library	Copy is edited/approved by numerous people
Specific topic assignments	Limited access to management for background
Bigger budgets and larger fees for super-quality writing	Greater difficulty accessing the "plant" level workers
	Greater challenge to make yourself indispensable, especially if client has a writers' stable

The possible advantages of a small company	The possible disadvantages of working with small clients
Fewer management tiers to navigate	Less sophisticated approach to communications
More streamlined approval process for copy	Lack of internal support in production
Writers can provide broader base of services	Lack of understanding about value of communications
Writers have more macro view of projects and business	Smaller budgets
	Nit-picking fee negotiations
Generalist writers play a more nurturing role throughout the editorial process, working with less experienced in-house people	Tighter deadlines
	A non-communications client may be noncommittal about projects
Writers can "educate" clients about mechanics of communications projects as well as the writers' value	
Opportunities to experiment with new writing and design options with the client	

The basics of this search and some key sources for it are listed later in this chapter. But first you need some kind of structured approach to making the search.

Keep It Manageable

Start with a list of ten top choices that you cull from your reading, preliminary research, and general knowledge. That number seems to be manageable for most people launching a search. Then, as you continue researching those companies further, you might find that some companies are not as financially stable as you'd like, or do not have the communications need for free-lancers. Then you ditch those choices and substitute other new companies at the bottom of the list.

This process allows the best targets to rise to the top. Any new ones would naturally start at the bottom. After a while, you might find that you have several lists working at once:

- A list—companies you've researched and are actively soliciting
- B list—companies that have free-lance needs you haven't explored yet
- C list—companies with solid financial pictures and appealing product lines but unclear communications needs
- D list—interesting companies you haven't yet investigated

As you research each one, you'll ferret out specific information that arms you for your direct solicitations. (More on that in Chapter VI, "Navigate the Marketing Maze.") Track down the following items or information if you can:

- Number of employees
- Location(s)
- Service or product lines
- Financial results from this and previous years
- Sales volume information
- A copy of the company's annual report
- Distribution channels and customer profile
- Regional, national, and/or global markets

- Names of individuals/company addresses/phone numbers
- Recent articles about the company

You won't necessarily find all this information about your targets, but this basic list should guide you through your research at the library, where you will refer to computerized as well as textual resources. Make friends with your reference librarians; they are an invaluable resource and your guardian angels.

One time I spent about two hours poring over computerized periodical listings for specific information about a couple of companies and came up dry. My frustration escalated because I had to relinquish the computer to another library patron. On my way out I offhandedly inquired with the reference librarian about the best way to track down this information. She smiled, swiveled around in her chair, picked up a large volume on the adjacent table, flipped open the book to a specific page, and handed it to me. There was all the information I needed.

Even the smallest, most remote libraries house tons of information about corporations. If yours doesn't have a specific resource, the librarian should be able to locate it, either by computer linkup or through the interlibrary lending system in force throughout the country. Most libraries will at least have access to the *State Manufacturer's Register,* which lists basic information about regional U.S. companies. Big-city libraries will have a host of company guides, often even narrowed to specific regions or by industry.

Here are some specific resources to hunt down at the library. While some are particular to the Chicago area, most large cities have similar texts about local companies. It is advisable to look at several sources, to give you a broad range of information and perspective about the companies you target.

Investext

This computer-based program alphabetically lists companies and any cross-referenced subjects related to those companies. Information summarized in this user-friendly program is often easier to digest than what you might find in an annual report. It's also right at your fingertips, on the library's easy-to-use computer system—no hunting through microfiche or library stacks for hard copies. And sometimes the listings refer to specific names of current staffers you might contact.

Marketing Directories

These directories publish names and additional information about companies in various major metropolitan areas, by county. For instance, the *Cook County Marketing Directory* lists detailed information about local companies in that Illinois county.

First Chicago Guide—aka "Becker" Guide

These one-page briefs of regional companies include sales figures, officers' names, product lines, balance sheet summaries, and income statements, sometimes charted over a period of time. Find out from your librarian if your city has a similar guide. This one is invaluable.

Metro [City] Major Employers

Information that would appeal to potential/interviewing employees. These directories are published around the country for different cities. They give you an insider's perspective that you won't see in most generic publications.

Fortune 500 Annual Reports

For writers fairly adept at sifting through an annual report, this is a good resource. Typically the library will have hard copies or microfiche copies on hand. According to Securities and Exchange Commission (SEC) law, any companies that offer their

stock publicly on an exchange must regularly file all their financial information.

That's how free-lancers and many other interested parties, such
as investors, can put these companies under the microscope and
decide if they are companies with which they should tango (or
tangle).

Included in these reports might also be a letter from the CEO, a
summary of key events that affected business productivity or stock-
holder interests during the previous year, a description of product
lines, the rationale for selling off or acquiring other companies, and
forecasts or long-term goals anticipated by the company.

Sometimes companies include some softer, public relations–
oriented pieces in the annual report, for example profiles of exem-
plary employees, progressive environmental activities initiated by
the company, and productivity programs launched corporate-wide
or individually within departments.

Get a Grip on Business Trends

While you're busy ironing out all the micro details of your marketing strategy and lining up your specific company targets, try to stay
on top of general economic and business trends—not just in
America but around the globe. Do it regularly, if for no other
reason than to look for new marketing opportunities. You just
don't know what piece of news could spawn an assignment.

While scanning the business section of our local town paper, I
came across an announcement about a seminar offered by a
communications association. I attended as a nonmember and
brought along my portfolio, business cards, and some extra samples. For the duration of the lecture, I sat next to a man who
happened to be an executive with a Fortune 500 company. We
got to talking, and the next thing I knew he was arranging for me
to complete a half-finished assignment that no one on staff had
time to finish.

After the lecture, I asked the speaker some questions, which also led to a future assignment.

There are some simple, practical ways to bone up on what is happening in the business community. You will never know what information might help you connect with a contact, prospect, or current client. I recommend reading several business periodicals and perusing the latest business books in print at your local bookstore. Here are some specific recommendations for writers:

- *The Wall Street Journal*
- The business section of your local paper
- Monthly periodicals that deal with personal and corporate finance, or business management concepts
- Local weekly business periodicals that detail what is happening in local commerce, e.g., Crain's publications
- Stock listings (at least weekly, if for no other reason than to see how a corporate client is doing)
- *The New York Times* Sunday business section—summarizes and analyzes big events in the business world
- *The New York Times* Sunday "Week in Review" section, a winner for broad perspective on the whys and wherefores of our changing world economy

What's Making the Global Economy Go Round

Political and economic upheaval of any sort can make, break, or alter an individual country's fragile balance. Think about the Berlin Wall falling, the breakup of the Soviet Union, coups in any country, and the continuing deterioration and human sacrifice in Bosnia. Many companies that set up shop in these areas have had to retrench, strategize for a longer haul, or even pull out.

Even orderly change in one country can have rippling effects on many other countries' economies and stability. Consider the transition to a new U.S. presidency, or trade pacts like the North American Free Trade Agreement (NAFTA), the attempts to squelch the organized crime stranglehold on the former Soviet Union's struggling free-enterprise system, or the lifting of U.S. trade restrictions with Vietnam.

Every day, each country's economy is linked more decisively with another's. This makes it incumbent on corporate communicators to understand the impact world events may have on an individual client. Understanding how the world's dynamics are changing gives your writing a three-dimensional perspective and enhances your services and value to clients.

How Corporations Communicate

Most companies churn out a steady flow of internal and external communications—in good times, in bad, even when buyouts or downsizing are about to do them in. Getting the news out is a matter of life and death for any company, regardless what that news may be.

As a free-lancer, you need to understand each company's communications philosophy and fit yourself into that context. Even if that approach says, "Communications has limited value," you can perhaps play a role in changing that mind-set.

Whether it be a simple memo between coworkers on an electronic mail system, a multimedia information campaign about a new benefits program, a quick-hit notice on a pay stub, or a letter from the company president explaining a strategic operations shift, communication makes change, growth, and understanding possible. And written communication forms the hub of most ventures within any company, even if the end product arrives via different media.

The ongoing "Excellence in Communications" study by the 11,500-member International Association of Business Communicators (IABC) proves how corporate America's progressive companies value communications. According to Gloria Gordon, the IABC's vice president of communications, the corporate executives surveyed for the study quantified that value, claiming they received back a 182 percent return on their investment for "a good communications manager."

"Companies that have an excellent reputation have found that they also have an excellent bottom line. Effective communications do this," says Gordon, who has worked at the association's San Francisco world headquarters for eleven years. "We've also seen our membership moving into management positions, as their value and prestige have grown."

Communications Gains Respect

As progressive companies and managers recognize the impact their words can have on others, many are attempting to produce them with more care.

"I don't use the words 'politically correct,' but I believe that being 'personally sensitive' is something that good communicators have to aspire to," says Larry Robbins, adjunct professor and director of the Communications program at the Wharton School, University of Pennsylvania. "The American workforce's multicultural population is having a very positive effect on communications internally, by causing people to think before they talk. If you realize that you may not be understood or may offend, then you plan better what you're going to communicate. This can only be good for the organization at large."

The growing role of communications in business is the byproduct of an evolving workplace, global economy, and society. According to Steven Ross, associate professor of Professional Practice at the Columbia University School of Journalism, there are avalanching forces compelling companies to respond and be responsive to their constituencies.

"The pressure is on to communicate—with issues of harassment, discrimination, liability issues," says the environmental activist and author/editor of fifteen books and three commercial software programs. "It's foolish for any company not to disclose information to its audiences, because we [reporters] can all get that information whether they want us to or not."

The trend toward leaner organizations that are more open and demand shared decision making with all employees is flourishing as more companies appreciate its direct correlation to increased productivity and profitability. Previously, the conventional mindset about communications in the corporate realm was that it was a frill. However, many companies learn the hard way that *not communicating* can be far more detrimental to an organization's health and longevity, especially during hard times.

"Whole layers of middle managers have disappeared, so whereas one manager might have had seven or eight people, now they have twenty people working for them," says Columbia's Ross, who has been with the university's journalism school part-time since 1973 and full-time since 1986. "Through all these workplace changes, there's a tremendous need to communicate with all these people. More stuff needs to be explained and there are fewer opportunities to communicate one on one."

A candid and networked communication channel from employees to management, management to employees, company to shareholders, and company to the community makes possible the new decision-sharing work strategy. This approach also seems to spawn more and more opportunities for free-lancers.

Antiquated Notions About Communications

Communicating used to be reserved for the womenfolk of a bygone era, who theoretically merely passed gossip, folk wisdom, and news over coffee. As long as corporate decision making remained strictly within the menfolk's purview, sharing information candidly throughout an organization was far from de rigueur. How the company worked, how managers made decisions, and how those decisions evolved were not shared with employees, the surrounding community, the media, or stockholders.

In the hierarchical, vertical, patriarchal corporate structures of yesteryear, management unilaterally made decisions and gave orders. And they traditionally didn't give a damn what employees thought about it.

Enter the topsy-turvy societal upheaval of the 1960s, Japanese managerial influences, and the high-tech revolution, and life forever changed from the boardroom down to the shop floor. More women and minorities entered the workforce, felt their untapped potential going to waste, and sought the education and on-the-job training necessary to win decision-making roles in the organization. Pink and blue were no longer the only dress code option for these workers.

Thirty years later, women and minorities are filtering into higher positions of power within corporate ranks and have fueled and accelerated the growing refusal of all employees to be mere sheep. All workers want their voices heard, acknowledged, and appreciated. They want to contribute to the organization that writes their paycheck.

And as companies solicit and value each individual's contribution more through upward and downward communication, each employee appreciates his or her own personal impact on the organization's productivity and future.

"The American corporate world needs to emphasize the importance of the individual, and collectively the organization can be more effective," says the Wharton School's Robbins. "Trust is built through communication, and good communication keeps companies out of trouble and helps bring a common understanding of corporate objectives to all employees."

At the same time, organizations are increasingly accepting the fact that employees are most productive when they are happy, treated well, and brought into the decision-making loop about operations and key corporate activities that affect their on-the-job performance.

"Open communication channels mean better productivity," Robbins continues, "because people feel a stake in the success of the organization and they enjoy better personal fulfillment knowing they're part of that success."

We're in This Together

I have witnessed that all communications—good and bad—affect the company's well-being. If information is passed on with indifference or lack of attention, it can jeopardize an organization's health. Produced with care, even bad news well explained can advance a company's future.

Progressive, profitable companies recognize the value of open communication lines among employees, management, and other stakeholders (stockholders, surrounding communities, and customers). This is borne out particularly during a down time or in the event of a crisis.

I have one client who struggles to get information out as expeditiously as possible to employees, so they don't read about it in the paper the next morning. This company also prepares any affected employees long in advance of the actual corporate change and eventual announcement to the press.

A well-oiled communications machine jumps into action to wrest control from the rumor mill that can destroy truth, deflate morale, and suppress profit. Look no further than the strategy chosen by the makers of Extra-Strength Tylenol during the notorious tampering incident in Chicago during the early 1980s.

Management averted a corporate disaster when it purged store shelves of its products, addressed media and public concerns openly, and offered rewards for any information leading to the arrest of the tampering offender. The company explained every move it made throughout the process, which not only eased the public's outrage, but also set the stage for the company's follow-up introduction of tamper-proof bottles.

"It's so important for [companies] to disclose everything up front and clearly. This isn't just to adhere to the letter of the law, but to explain their policies, reasons, and products to the community, their constituencies and customers," says Robbins. "This goodwill has a good deal to do with being good citizens and it adds to the value of the corporation. There has always been goodwill advertising, but now, companies that are the most appreciated are the ones that don't hide things."

During normal, noncrisis work periods, far-thinking companies want all parts of the company synchronized, in harmony. Internally, this means that all employees:

- Understand their given job responsibilities
- See where they fit into the corporate matrix
- Understand their internal and external "customers"
- Appreciate their individual value to the corporation
- Know that management respects their contributions
- Know they will be rewarded for their successes

This prescription for corporate success, sometimes known loosely as "employee ownership," has salvaged many a company with sluggish ledgers and been the entrenched long-term philosophy of some of the most profitable. Robert Waterman and Jim Peters explain this "productivity through people" concept in their timeless best-seller *In Search of Excellence*.

"Treat people as partners; treat them with dignity; treat them with respect. Treat them—not capital spending and automation—as the primary source of productivity gains . . . If you want productivity and the financial award that goes with it, you must treat your workers as your most important asset."[1]

[1] Robert Waterman and Thomas Peters, *In Search of Excellence* (New York: Harper-Collins, 1980), p. 238.

A 1990 report from *Business Marketing* magazine also high-lighted the importance of this concept to any company's ability to produce quality services or products and to satisfy the customer. "Quality can only happen when every single person involved understands it, believes in it and makes it a part of everything they do."

As in any relationship, this success is possible only when all parties understand one another. That's possible only with clear communications up and down the strata of any company: face-to-face communications, in newsletters, brochures, employee annual reports, videotapes, computer-based communications systems, and audiotapes.

Companies that respect this kind of internal and external candor bring this to all their communications. This is where you come in. It is incumbent on any free-lancer to understand how each prospective or existing client values communications, even if your objective is only to get a feeling for how the company commits financial and time resources to communications efforts.

Ideally, your goal should also be to incorporate this knowledge into your correspondence and dealings with the client, and then mirror the company's approach to communications in your own writing.

Regardless of whether you background yourself this way for an existing or prospective client, this understanding will go a long way to making you a more appealing and valued free-lancer. Leverage this knowledge as you begin nailing down inside contacts within your target companies. The next chapter will help you with that process.

Chapter VI

Navigate the Marketing Maze

ONCE YOU ESTABLISH a hit list of target companies and complete a thorough library investigation of the targets' financial status and corporate structure, it's time to make contact. Your top objectives early on should be to sort out:

- Which of my target companies use free-lancers?
- Who are the decision-makers?
- How does each company delegate communications responsibilities?

Your target list will evolve and solidify as you gather more and more information about each company's communications people, philosophy, and free-lance policies. To make this process work most effectively, you need to:

- Allot a specific time each day to make calls
- Make anonymous initial contacts
- Know what questions to ask
- Build rapport with "gatekeepers"
- Embrace cold calling as your ally
- Time your prospective-client calls strategically
- Blend your assets/background into conversations
- Maintain an upbeat attitude

Making headway within each target organization is actually the toughest part of your job as a free-lancer, because it requires basic, at-the-source investigating that only you can do. But keep in mind that all these telephone inquiries are the best and sometimes only way for you to market yourself to many corporate clients.

Reach Out and Get in Touch

Your first objective during this early part of your marketing is to discover which companies use free-lancers and who within the company does the hiring. This may take one phone call or possibly a series of calls—repeat initial calls, follow-up calls, and referral calls—depending on how each company delegates its communications responsibilities and how each contact responds to you. So buckle up at your desk with that target list, your phone, and a legal pad in front of you.

Prepare yourself for the initiation rite of calling switchboards and receptionists to nail down names, titles, and some skeleton organizational information.

Expect to allot a specific time every day for making these calls, say an hour between 7 and 10 A.M., until you have a solid list of contacts and some work assignments coming in. You will need this discipline throughout the life of your business, so start making it a simple, no-stress habit now. At some point, you can probably whittle that marketing time down to one hour each on two weekdays, for example. But, one way or the other, you must do it regularly.

This chore may seem like drudgery, but the time will fly if you start making inroads with anyone at your target companies. As you fill that legal pad with all kinds of phone numbers, contact names, titles and department names, you'll be building a potential client list and market niche for yourself.

After one hour, some targets may blossom, stay in limbo, or cease to be options completely. Don't be disappointed if you make tremendous headway with one target but get not a hint of response from any others on your list. You never know who is going to answer the phone or what type of information you will uncover in these initial fact-finding missions.

After your hour is up, you will want to complete any follow-up letter writing, samples package mailing, or referral calls gleaned from these first efforts. Your marketing time on any given day might vary from one hour of calls only, to one hour of calls and several hours writing follow-up letters and preparing and sending out sample packages of your work.

But before we get into follow-up procedures (covered thoroughly in Chapter VII, "Follow Up in Style"), let's talk about how those preliminary conversations might go.

Making Contact

An anonymous phone call to a main number sometimes turns out to be an informational gold mine. That is, if you happen to get a human instead of an automated voice-mail system.

If all you have is a central number, then call it. Your first question might be as simple as: "Hi, could you tell me who heads up communications for the company?" Make sure you ask a question that requires an answer, or the operator may just connect you to any old human before you have enough information to proceed. There are many possible responses to such a question. They all tell you something about the company. Here are some of the responses I've encountered:

1. *"For which department [operating group, business unit]?"*
This indicates that communications functions are probably decentralized to each operating group or department, which means you have some further investigation to do.

2. *"Jane Doe is the manager of Communications. Would you like me to connect you?"*
While this tells you the company's communications are probably centralized, you most likely do not want to get connected

immediately with that person. Definitely do not opt for a voice-mail message to that person, no matter what the operator suggests. It is too early.

You should respond with another question, such as: "Who works for Jane Doe?" or "Who heads up publications?" If the operator is a kind soul and does not have some call-timing averages to maintain, he or she will probably be able to give you a few more names. The operator might respond by saying, "Allan Dowrite manages internal public relations and Suzie Liaison handles external public relations."

Then she or he will want to boot you off the line or connect you. So, thank him or her for the information, and write down any names, titles, and numbers on your legal-pad target list for an extended cold-calling blitz the next day perhaps.

3. *"Communications are directed from our parent company in New York. Would you like that number?"*

This response tells you that you will start the same process over again with the switchboard in New York.

4. *"Is this a media call?"*

This kind of response might be sending a couple different messages: The company likes to control anyone going through their communications system. Or perhaps they're embroiled in some big public relations brouhaha. One way or the other, turn on the charm and do not let them hang up before you have some information:

"Oh, why no. I'm just trying to find out a few things about the company's communications department."

What Do You Need to Know?

Talk to as many people as you can without actually giving your name or having to confront the decision-makers at this time. What you are trying to do is amass as much background about these companies as you can before you actually solicit work.

If you come to the inevitable critical conversations with lots of information in your arsenal, you won't waste a decision-maker's time asking questions that could have been answered by an assistant or even an operator. Instead, you'll cut to the chase and discuss what role free-lancers actually play within that company. Eventually, you want the following questions answered:

- Who heads up communications work for the company?
- What types of communications projects does the department do?
- How many people are in the department (if it's centralized)?
- How does each department delegate its communications responsibilities?
- What kinds of projects, if any, do free-lancers complete?
- Will it be possible for me to set up an interview time?
- Is it possible to obtain some samples of publications or brochures produced by the company? How about an annual report (if it's not a public company)?
- Who is in charge of each area within communications?

In your preliminary conversations with assistants, secretaries, or other gatekeepers, you may get a helpful, knowledgeable person on the phone who does not mind filling you in about the company. Generally, you will not want to tell the gatekeepers immediately your name and your business, but if you sense they will offer you more information if you explain who you are, then be flexible and launch an abbreviated spiel: "I'm a free-lance writer and I'm just trying to find out who handles those assignments, or if the company uses outside writers at all."

You might be surprised how much information you can get. Handle these conversations delicately with an approach of "I'm just seeking information." That seems to keep people on the line longer.

If a company does not use free-lancers at all, then your search at that company possibly stops here after only one phone call. It's also possible that a gatekeeper might have misunderstood your inquiry and slotted you as someone looking for full-time work. This could land you in a conversation with Personnel, which rarely hires free-lancers for communications, unless it's a very small company.

I have also discovered that even if a company flatly denies using free-lancers, it may have a use for one in the future. If a gatekeeper tells you point-blank that they don't use free-lancers, that may be only part of the story.

It's always possible the decision-makers do hire free-lancers from time to time, but it's just not common office knowledge. Some company contacts will tell you it's unusual for them to hire contract writers, but they may suggest you send samples. This can never hurt; think of it as an investment or practice in writing cover letters and arranging your samples.

Dealing with Gatekeepers

People I like to call "gatekeepers" will handle most of your preliminary phone calls. These are receptionists, secretaries, and co-workers, who can block or facilitate your contact with the target decision-maker. Conversations with gatekeepers don't have to be antagonistic, confrontational, or problematic, however. Use these opportunities to illuminate yourself and build relationships within the ranks of each company you contact.

Coworkers can sometimes impede your progress and access to decision-makers more than any other interceptor. They may take one of several unprofessional actions when they receive your call. They may not take a message at all; write down incomplete information; take it upon themselves to pre-interview you; shunt your call through to the decision-maker at a bad time; or give you wrong information about the company's policy toward free-lancers.

All in all, you are better off dealing with the professional gatekeepers. Secretaries and receptionists are professionally trained to intercept calls and take accurate messages, which allows their bosses to work undisturbed by most unsolicited outside calls. Extend yourself personally with the intermediary people; they can help you carve a path to the decision-maker's door.

The gatekeepers "protect" the decision-makers and can spell life or death for your success with the company, no matter who sits in the inner sanctum. In order to connect with these people, apply basic courtesies to your many conversations:

- Be diplomatic, unpretentious, unpatronizing, and nice (read empathetic). Always make it clear that you really need their help.
- Acknowledge the help they do give you.
- Never demand information or materials.
- Sincerely acknowledge something unique about them—that they are in the office far earlier than their coworkers, or that they have an unusual voice, or they are easy to work with.
- Be genuine with these people; they will sniff out the hogwash.
- Pump them casually for information while you are talking with them.

If you are not making any headway getting through to the boss, or the gatekeeper will not plug you through after two calls from you, then it is time to assertively solicit the gatekeeper's help. Tell him or her that you want the straight dope: Does the boss ever use free-lance writers or should you talk to someone else?

I have been amazed at how effective a last-ditch, candid SOS to a gatekeeper can be. This approach must be rehearsed, planned, and calmly executed. Try the following approach:

WRITER: Look, Susan, can you help me out here. I'm sorry to keep bugging you, but what's the best way for me to get in touch with Ms. Writeon?

I left several messages over the last two weeks, when you

said she was out of town. Now she's on vacation for ten days and probably already threw out my messages from before. What do you think? Should I just wait or should I send her my samples anyway?

SEC'Y: Right. I'm sorry you've had so many miscommunications. She did get the messages, I'm sure of it because I handed them to her after we talked last week. I know you wanted to get through to her.

WRITER: So, what do you think? Maybe she just isn't looking for any free-lancers right now? Or was this just an odd time?

SEC'Y: I can't tell you if she needs anyone now. She'll have to tell you that. But I know one thing, Ms. Writeon is always looking at new writers' samples. As a matter of fact, someone was just in here the other day. I still have his stuff on my desk to send back to him.

WRITER: So, what do you suggest I do now?

These kinds of conversations help you build a rapport with gatekeepers. And you might even nail down some interesting information about the prospect's approach with free-lancers. It cannot hurt to show a little of your frustration to this person, who is a working person, too, and understands you are only trying to put bread on the table. Solicit help and see what happens.

Cold Calling: The Free-Lancer's Ace

If you master the art of cold calling and follow-up calls, you will have a decided advantage in the free-lance market. Many writers, out of fear, do not give cold calling a fair shot. They feel too embarrassed to ask for work over the phone, or they fear rejection. You need to come to terms with this or you could stymie your free-lance success.

Cold calling really *is* easier to do than you think. Many laypeople and writers are shocked to discover that this is how I first landed the majority of my clients. It appears too rough, inelegant, un-professional, or confrontational. I believe it is the best way to land work, because you are going right to the source and facing the would-be client one-on-one.

So do not let the term "cold calling" scare you. Consider that you will warm up by talking to possibly several layers of initial contacts before you reach the decision-makers. This should arm you with a lot of information as well as practice talking to miscellaneous company people.

Keep in mind a few things:

- Many corporate communications people are accustomed to dealing with free-lance solicitations; your call will not seem unusual.
- If they do use free-lancers, they'll have guidelines to relate to you.
- Since you are communicating by phone, the client can't see your potentially red face or sweaty palms.
- At the end of each of these initial calls, you will either be happy it ended or elated that you have a foot in the door.

Timing Is Key

My rule of thumb is this: Begin calling early in the morning, around 7 A.M. I'm no longer surprised by the number of people I discover at work that early. One of my clients commented that her company was readjusting the starting time on the corporate date book's daily entries to 6 or 7 A.M., since many employees had complained that their days began much earlier than 8 A.M.

I just accept that if a client arrives at work early, then I need to work within that person's schedule.

You will find out quickly how early a company's communications people begin working in the mornings and how late they stay at the office working at night. You will also find out whether regional or industry-specific work attitudes affect this potential client's hours.

For instance, the communications people for a multinational company based in Denver might come in early to handle calls from its New York and European offices. On the other hand, marketing people at a local insurance office in town may open for business at 8:30 A.M. at the earliest and turn on the night line at 4:30 P.M. Try to gauge ahead of time how each customer might operate.

You might also find that different people within the same department operate on individual "time zones." One of my client companies has a communications head who works late (until around 7:30 P.M.), so she comes in later in the morning, after dropping her kids off at school and day care. One of her employees, my immediate contact person, typically hustles into work at 6:45 A.M., hangs up her coat, turns on the lights and coffee machine, and hits the computer by 7:15 A.M.

Here are a few reasons for calling early:

- You might reach the contact directly, since many department heads are early starters.
- The office is quiet.
- Secretaries are not as likely to be around early to intercept calls.
- The contact is alert and ready to attack the day.
- The contact is not already swamped in several things.
- An early-morning person will be more receptive to another early-morning go-getter's solicitations.
- Even if the contact cannot talk to you at length right then, you should be able to set up another time to talk at his or her convenience.

Here is how a possible conversation might go with an early-morning contact. Let's assume you know a few things about the company, as well as the person's name, title, general responsibilities. You first need to find out if he or she uses free-lancers, then quickly establish some credentials and company specifics without becoming a pest to the contact.

CONTACT: XYZ Company. This is Jane Liaison.

FREE-LANCER: Good morning, Jane. This is Maryclaire Collins. I think you're just the person I need to talk to . . . Do you still head up internal public relations?

CONTACT: That's right. What can I do for you?

FREE-LANCER: Well, I'm a free-lance writer. I do work for the Makeshift Corp., SecondBest Inc., and HighPriceGuys Ltd. and I'm trying to track down who hires free-lancers at XYZ.

CONTACT: Actually, I do. But we don't have any assignments right now. You can send me a résumé and some samples if you like. I have several people who write for me regularly, but I'm always looking around.

FREE-LANCER: Great. I've been doing some free-lance writing on a safety management project for ABC Company and I recently read that XYZ is also launching a big safety management program. Are you using outside writers to handle any of the communications for that?

CONTACT: I just assigned someone last week. Too bad you didn't call then. Who else have you written for?

FREE-LANCER: Well, besides Makeshift, SecondBest, and HighPriceGuys, I just wrote an orientation video script for the Crankcase Corp., and I'm working on food ingredient brochures for Gonebad, Inc. I also regularly contribute to NitPick Inc.'s management magazine. I have several samples I could show you.

CONTACT: So you've written for other food companies as well. I tell you what. Why don't you come in today or tomorrow so I can look over your samples? How about noon? I'll have a break then.

FREE-LANCER: Great. I'll be there. Just tell me what floor your office is on.

At this point, you do not quibble over the specific time, unless you have an important conflicting appointment at the same hour. Make your schedule fit around any new contact who is going to the trouble to meet with you in person, unless you are truly facing sickness, death, or an irreversible appointment. Do not bring up your scheduling problems with racquetball, kids, dogs, or baby-sitters.

You want potential clients to feel that they are a top priority and that you are wholly concentrating on them when you need to be. You especially want to communicate this single-minded dedication at the beginning of your relationship, so they feel they can count on you.

Naturally this conversation will go a little differently if you haven't accumulated as much experience as I claimed to have in the preceding conversation. However, if you have followed my approach for targeting clients, you'll have a solid idea why this is a good company for you to write for and why you'll be a good fit with them anyway. You'll also know what specific background assets you bring to the table. During your conversations, blend in your knowledge of the company and your own assets in the following priority order:

- Specific projects you have completed for that exact company
- Specific, germane projects you have completed for other companies
- Specific writing experience for that industry or that topic
- Specific, germane trade or consumer-writing experience
- Any experience working for similar companies
- General writing experience for any companies
- General trade or consumer-writing experience
- Specific professional knowledge of that industry
- Industry-specific or general business writing during internships at the college or graduate level

The Right Attitude

Regardless of how conversations go on the phone, I operate on the assumption that if the company uses free-lancers at all, then they will want to see my stuff.

I base this on my historical success rate, which dictates the following: About half the time, my target companies will be or have been in the market for free-lance help; about 90 percent of the time those targets will want to see my samples, résumé, and client list. Out of that group I can typically expect to land assignments from about half. So, overall, I generate business from about 20 to 25 percent of my original target companies.

Knowing this helps me attack my targets with some confidence. And once you have begun cranking out copy for several companies, you then have references and credibility to back up your confidence and portfolio. Of course, it's not always so easy to stay optimistic. You may go through marketing droughts that have no correlation to any economic trend or forecast. You need to think ahead and constantly hone your approach to new and old contacts.

Generally, you should try to project a self-assured, successful, confident attitude in all your work relationships. Even during the inevitable downswings of your business cycle, check any desperate or begging impulses at your client's door. Nagging a client or gatekeeper for information or business might permanently discolor their opinion of you.

Getting to the Right Person

While you're busy figuring out who heads up communications and whether the company uses free-lancers at all, keep in mind that the department head isn't necessarily the person who will actually hire you. That's the person I keep referring to as the "decision-maker."

You may eventually deal with a department head or a vice president of communications, but many times your fate with a given company will lie in the hands of someone below the executive level.

So if you're researching your target companies and see that a company lists a vice president or director of communications, marketing, or public affairs in a marketing directory, just file away that information. Jot down that person's name and number on the target list of companies you culled from library, word-of-mouth, and periodical sources. It's good to etch as many names in your memory banks as possible, so you'll recognize these names when they pop up in the consumer press or in your dealings with other corporate staffers. Consider this information a head start, or at least a small piece of information possibly telling you that the company:

- Values communications enough to name someone a vice president of the department
- Is so big it requires an officer in charge of the department
- Has centralized several operational responsibilities under a communications umbrella

In your preliminary phone calls to a company, I don't recommend ringing up a vice president of corporate communications to ask for work right off the bat. This is not the person who typically cranks out and assigns communications projects day-to-day, so calling this person first could slow down your hunt. At best, this officer may shunt off your call or message to one of her or his foot soldiers. And that person may feel slighted you didn't start with him or her—the decision-maker—the person who hires and fires the free-lancers.

At worst, a top officer may toss out your message. That's OK; it is still too early for you to attempt a tête-à-tête with the top dog. As a matter of fact, you may never have any contact with this person at all, even after you are an established free-lancer for a given company.

How Do Your Targets Divvy Up Communications?

You need to identify whether each company's communications organization is centralized or decentralized, or a hybrid, in order to market yourself most efficiently and land assignments. This information will give you a springboard for understanding how communications assignments will be doled out to outsiders, how you will have to work within the company's structure, and how this structure will affect your dealings with internal communications people. This sets the course for your future relationship with any given company, and will direct your future actions looking for work from and/or completing assignments for internal clients.

Keep in mind throughout the following discussion that either structure works for both large and small companies.

Communicating from a Core

Some companies have communications *centralized* in one department with one core staff of people dedicated to completing or at least overseeing communications projects and assignments for every operating group.

Large companies may even take this centralized organization further, by dedicating communications liaisons, account executives, or coordinators to each operating unit. These people will coordinate their departments' communications needs in collaboration with corporate communications staff, which relies on the liaisons' expertise in technical areas and trains them in consistent corporate standards for communication.

Centralized functions make a free-lancer's marketing job a little easier. Hunting down communications decision-makers is simpler when one in-house group coordinates public relations, public affairs, publications, speeches, A/V productions, media affairs, and meeting planning.

You may also discover that these in-house people are truly communications experts or professionals, hired specifically because they have hands-on experience with the gamut of media options and can adapt their skills to a variety of industries, projects, and operations.

On the other hand, many of these centralized departments are understaffed and rife with underpaid, overworked communicators who probably wish they could switch places with you. Keep several things in mind as you deal with staffers from a big-company communications department:

- They are usually very busy. (They need your help badly if they have hired you.)
- They rarely have time to chat. (Do not waste their time.)
- They see a lot of free-lancers come through the doors. (You are expendable.)
- They are used to high-quality performance from people inside and outside the department. (You and your work will be scrutinized.)
- They like continuity of writing style in their publications. (If you make the cut with these people, you will have a great sinecure.)
- They expect writers to get up to speed quickly on many subjects. (Learn the company's business and industry environment.)

Because a centralized department generally controls, oversees, or at least operates as a central archive for all the company's communication projects, it is essential for you to make the grade with this department first.

No matter how big the company is, it will be hard for you to obtain more assignments with any other department if you do not live up to the editorial and operating standards of central communications unit staffers, or you do not get along with them. These departments rightfully covet the communications control they have struggled to attain over the years.

The message here is: *Work with the system.*

A client once told me she had recommended me to a colleague of hers at another company. It turned out I had free-lanced for this company in the past, but not for this particular person. Unwittingly, I thought I'd save a few extra steps and bypass the company's centralized communications department. I called this woman directly to establish contact and solicit work.

Although *she* was enthusiastic about my possible involvement in a particular project she had in the works, she suggested that I should first go through corporate communications. I said thanks and decided to follow up.

Unfortunately, my action came too late. Corporate communications got wind of this initial contact, and I received a scorching message from the communications manager I had worked with before. The manager reprimanded me about contacting other departments and informed me that she had already lined up another free-lancer for the project.

Far-Flung Communications

Other companies *decentralize* communications by giving autonomy to business operating units to control communications in their own way.

Although it can be more complicated to find a niche with a company with decentralized functions, there are always new people to try if you hit a dead end in one operating unit of the company. A free-lancer can knock on many doors without stepping on too many toes as he or she solicits work within one organization.

Your role as a communicator can be invaluable to a company that delegates communications individually by department.

Sometimes you will find that the communications person is actually an operations person who had the additional responsibilities dumped on him or her by management. If these operations personnel are in charge of the area by default, and in addition to normal workday responsibilities in another area, they may not have the experience, skills, flair, or enthusiasm for the job that dedicated communications people in a centralized department will be expected to have.

One way or the other, while tracking down these people may mean a lot of phone-tag forays, it is worth the struggle. Once you have bitten off a chunk of business in one operational area of a decentralized company, you should try to leverage that for more business in another area. Contrast this situation, which offers multiple chances to generate business all under one roof, with the one-shot-only chance you might have with a centralized company. It is worth the extra phoning effort up front.

Finding contacts at a decentralized company is just a matter of defining the company operating structure and working your way (via telephone contacts) through each group to see which ones use or need free-lance writers in communications.

Sometimes it can be difficult to obtain the company's organizational information. Occasionally potential clients have let me look at printed organizational charts during courtesy interviews. If that is not possible, however, most people will be willing to give you some basic structural information over the phone.

If you are asked by a contact why you need this information, just say that you are a free-lance writer and need to know who is in charge of communications for each division. Even in these anonymous conversations, you should be able to obtain at least one or two names, to give you a start.

Frequently in a decentralized organization, one communications person in one division will suggest you call his or her counterpart in a different division. If he or she does not offer this, feel free to ask for more referrals.

Some of the sweetest words you will hear are the following:

"Call so-and-so, he's looking for someone to write the department's [orientation video, brochure, panel script, newsletter] pronto. Here's his number."

Never hesitate to ask for referrals in a decentralized environment, especially if your first contacts do not have any assignments to hand out at the time you call. According to my corporate survey, referrals tied for first place as being the best way to gain access to a client.

Still other companies structure a *hybrid organization*. Individual departments and operating groups control their own communications responsibilities, but they're backed up by a centralized communications department. That home-office staff of communications professionals might head up corporate-wide projects and review all communications for conformity to corporate standards.

So, while each department determines its own communications budgets and needs, the centralized communications department keeps a firm rein on what information and communications are being distributed. Often, the centralized staff will collaborate with the operational communicators on given projects, sharing their collective expertise to produce the most effective communications possible.

During all these phone calls, you'll be accumulating a lot of new information—phone numbers, names, titles, department organization—that you'll be adding to your original target list of ten companies. Now you need to incorporate all that information neatly into a revised list, keeping in mind that you'll be reorganizing it to reflect your target companies' business potential.

Chapter VII

Follow Up in
Style

YOU NEED TO MAKE your target list work for you. Otherwise, you better have a fabulous memory if you plan just to keep scratching new information all over your first list. Instead, simplify your life. Retype the list after each time you launch a phone-calling spree.

This should be a simple enough procedure if you have a personal computer and a decent printer. Just plug your handwritten changes into the computer version of your target-list document, put the date at the top, and print a new copy for yourself. Then, clip the new typed list on top of the old one (that includes the handwritten notations) or file the old one. Don't throw it away.

You need to keep a copy of every target-list version, in case you need to refer back to some number or company name that you thought was obsolete at the time you shelved it. This also gives you a chronological history of your marketing efforts, which you can refer to if you're analyzing or rethinking your approach. The information may stay fresh in your brain for a few weeks or months, but two years down the road you may not remember who those previous contacts were.

As you re-sort the list, use some common sense. Cross off the companies that definitely do not use free-lancers at all, and then order the rest this way:

1. Companies that *do* use free-lancers and show interest in you
2. Companies that sometimes use free-lancers and show mild enthusiasm for seeing your stuff

3. Companies about which you have a lot of background information but no specific leads
4. Companies with centralized communications that you haven't pursued yet
5. Companies with decentralized communications that you haven't pursued yet
6. Companies that have not used outside writers but asked you to send samples for their files anyway

When you return to your marketing-list file later, it will be clear which targets hold the most promise. You won't waste any valuable marketing time trying to refresh your memory.

As the List Grows

As you accumulate significantly more than ten companies on the main list, I recommend reorganizing them into the four priority lists outlined on page 70, Chapter V, "Find Your Corporate Niche." Group your ongoing solicitations under these general A, B, C, and D categories, which distinguish between companies you're actively soliciting and others you're interested in investigating. I like to keep these four types in separate files, for the sake of organization and handling ease.

The same goes for any companies that actually ask you to bid on an assignment. They have earned a separate file folder. You want to keep your marketing efforts segregated from your actual hits and in-person presentations or bid situations. In addition, I like to write up a card for my alphabetized Rolodex that includes internal contact names, titles, addresses, and phone numbers. Then, after I've submitted a bid, talked with contacts on the phone, presented my portfolio, or landed an assignment, I note the date of each event with a one- or two-word description of what happened (e.g., 4/14 sent bid).

Up Close and Personal

If a client asks you to come in for a presentation, you are on the road to landing that client. This is your chance to strut your stuff, both written and personal. Even if you have sent prospective clients some samples by mail, they may still want to review your full portfolio at a first meeting. The more the portfolio displays an aesthetically appealing, well-calculated, thorough sample of your work, the more impressive it—and you—will be.

During these meetings, it's actually wise to lead the client through the samples yourself. Don't leave the viewing to the client's discretion, if you can avoid it. Turn the portfolio to face your client and stop at appropriate pieces. This helps you control the situation and keep the prospect focused on what you decide is important. Of course, if the prospect asks if you have written about something specific as you are guiding her or him through your samples, take a moment to locate a pertinent sample. Then continue where you left off.

But having a slick portfolio, a beautiful résumé, and a clever business card is not enough. Part of selling you, your portfolio, and your versatility is to make sure the "wrapping" is as professional looking as the comprehensive portfolio being presented. That means you need to scrutinize your appearance.

Before you ever set foot in a prospect's door, scrutinize your corporate wardrobe. If you work out of the house, you might not have checked out, much less purchased, the latest in chic business attire. This is not the time for a major investment, but it is time to analyze your look vis à vis what might be considered de rigueur at the prospect's company.

You want to look like a creative person, but you do not necessarily want "avant-garde" embossed on your forehead. After all, these people will be trying to visualize you talking to their chief executive officer, in addition to other company people up and down the ranks.

Think about the following basics:

- A fresh, stylish haircut
- A clean or professionally pressed suit/outfit
- Solid color dresses or shirts; wild prints are distracting.
- For women: no need for traditional suits, unless it is a very conservative company. Just take a cue from your clients. No low-cut tops or extremely short skirts.
- For men: basic gray and blue suits, sport coat, and complementary pants. Nothing too flashy. You cannot go wrong with traditional attire. Ties are a good idea.
- Appropriate dress shoes.

Although "success dressing" is covered ad nauseam in job-hunting guides, newspaper and magazine features, you might not think of this particular aspect of work as critical to a free-lancer's success. As unfortunate as it may be, many people in the corporate environment will unconsciously or consciously judge us by how we look, dress, and act, in addition to how we write.

I like to think of this aspect of my work in a more positive, challenging spirit. In my mind it shows a certain personal flexibility to be able to switch from the "topsiders-jeans-ponytail" look at my computer one day to my "heels-blazer-briefcase" look at a client's office the next day, and my "work boots-khakis-gloves" look for a client's mine tour the day after that.

Before you arrive at your appointment, rehearse what situations or questions might present themselves at this particular prospect's workplace. For example:

- Will you interview company officers in their offices?
- Will you attend group meetings with managers or plant-level people?

- Will you tour a factory to research and to interview line workers?
- Will you spend several days or a weekend at a managers' conference that might include golf or "informal" cocktails?
- Will you have to go to trade shows with a client?
- Will you field-produce the recorded segments of an orientation video?

Thinking about these different situations should alert you to the variety of dress, attitude, demeanor, and journalistic technique you might employ. And rehearsing any situation will boost your confidence and morale.

The Follow-Up Letter

Once you've met with a client, even if you have not secured an assignment, you should send a follow-up letter. And in order to seal a deal or keep yourself in the prospect's mind, you need to perfect your follow-up correspondence with clients. Three typical times you might send letters are:

- After a meeting when you bid on a project
- After a meeting when you land a specific assignment
- After an introductory, courtesy meeting with no concrete assignments discussed

Sample letters for these occasions follow.

The easiest to write are the first two, when you have your teeth into an assignment. The prospect apparently likes your work well enough either to ask you to bid on a project or actually fulfill an assignment. Great! In the bid letter, you clearly thank the prospect for this opportunity and briefly restate your credentials without being overly ingratiating or self-aggrandizing. After all, you had your opportunity to pitch yourself earlier. Just bring yourself back into the client's focus succinctly, then get into the guts of your bid.

The second type of letter, when you are restating your responsibilities for a given assignment, is a little trickier. Although you are seemingly just summarizing the assignment scope, drafts, hours, fees, and so on, you are also showing the client how well you listened, how well you understand the customer's needs, and how conscientious you are about your business.

The toughest to write are those that follow a preliminary presentation, extensive phone inquiry, or other first critical contact with corporate prospects. This is your second, and sometimes last, chance to remind a prospective client who you are and what you can do for him or her. The letter must first thank the client for whatever information he or she revealed to you about the company, then reiterate what, if any, conclusions came from your meeting, and finally subtly restate what your potential value might be to this client. It also does not hurt to mention any connections (personal and professional) you two might have in common.

Never dash off any follow-up letters to clients. Each letter and each client calls for careful attention to tone, clarity, and a distinct projection of you, the writer. These letters must be printed on your best letterhead stationery with a business card enclosed.

Sample Letter #1—After Bidding at a Presentation

(For more information about determining on-the-spot bids, please see Chapter VIII, "The Question of Fees.")

Client
Company
Address

Dear Elaine,

Thanks so much for the chance to bid on the three brochures
you're producing for your sales force. The fact that you had
so much information about the project made it easy for me to
give you an estimate on the spot. I don't always have the luxury of working under those conditions.

I just wanted to confirm what we talked about yesterday at the
meeting and also to extend a "volume" discount. For quite a
while now I've been interested in working with your marketing
team, so I hope this additional offer sweetens the package.

You mentioned you'd like to assign all three (4-panel) brochures to one writer, if the right person and most economical
offer comes along. I told you at the meeting that based on my
rates I could complete the project for between $2,800 and
$3,400. I stick by that original estimate and want you to
know that my final invoices never exceed my bid range, and
many times actually end up lower. In this case, I'd also like to
extend a 10 percent discount on the total invoice, as long as
you assign me all three brochures.

My services will entail the same items we discussed
yesterday—researching, outlining, a first draft, a rewrite, and
some production coordination. I built time for all those com-
ponents into my bid price. Anyway, give me a call after you
think this over. I'm looking forward to hearing your decision.

Yours truly,

Queenie Free-lance
Write-on, Inc.

Sample Letter #2—After Landing an Assignment

Client
Company
Address

Dear Fred,

Thank you for faxing all that background information to me so promptly. That will certainly jump-start my research. I merely need to set up an appointment with your corporate library to complete the target search.

I just wanted to write and confirm everything we talked about during the meeting, mostly to refresh my memory about the assignment and to tip you off to any new concerns we should discuss.

My assignment is to script-write a video "identity brochure" for the company's computer services division. It will incorporate information about the department's new organization, its revamped services and new customer orientation. You expect this video to have an external as well as internal audience, so I have to stay away from too much corporate jargon and acronyms.

I'll be using a voice-over narrator to pull together all the sound bites from your in-house people. I also plan to meet with your computer graphics people to see what visuals they're creating.

Sometime early next week I'll fax you a rough draft. Call me or fax back any changes. I'm sure we'll be talking before then.

Sincerely,

Almost A. Spielberg
Videos 'R' Us

Sample Letter # 3—After a Presentation Meeting

Client
Company
Address

Dear Suzi,

It was a pleasure meeting with you last Tuesday. Thanks so much for the plant tour. The photos in the last issue of your corporate magazine do not do justice to the facility's size or sophistication.

It was also an unexpected plus to meet Hilary Bigboss and see the new management publication you and she produce. Your department has its hands full with that and the four quarterly customer publications XYZ produces. It's an impressive public relations exposure that's apparently working—at least according to last week's *Wall Street Journal* mention.

I'm excited about the prospect of working on any of your publications, although I understand no assignments are open right now. Keep me in mind for the future. With my experience writing for manufacturing companies, I think I could tackle any stories—particularly complex marketing ones—you have coming up.

I'll call you again in a month to check in and see if anything new is cooking. I'll be in the area at another client's office next week. Could I take you out to lunch? I'll call and see if we can work something out.

Thanks again to you and Hilary.

Yours truly,

Marty McKissup
WordsWork, Inc.

Chapter VIII

The Question of Fees

FOR SOME OF US, the cold call and personal interview are less daunting than the discussion of fees. Free-lancers can use a variety of approaches for setting and negotiating fees with clients, but regardless of which approach you use, you must be prepared to discuss money with confidence.

Successfully and painlessly negotiating fees and customizing a fee structure for each client requires flexibility and creativity. Although you want to present your fee structure in an objective way, you need to know in the back of your mind that you will adapt it to the client.

This does not mean you should equivocate when talking about your fees, but be prepared to change your approach with different clients. Intransigence on the money issue could keep you from a given assignment or even a long-term future with a first-time client. So be ready to adapt.

Typically, free-lancers operate on a "set fee," "hourly rate," or "hybrid" approach.

Before you agree to complete an assignment, even if you are desperate for the work, you must come to all meetings prepared to talk money. Never act as if you had not even thought about the bucks involved, or you will look inexperienced at best, and you will be taken advantage of at worst. Never accept an assignment without knowing how you will charge this client and the approximate compensation you will expect to receive.

If this approach seems calculating and "unartistic," try to

remember you are in this to make money; it is a business and your livelihood. You have to take the time to sit down and define what your services are worth in financial terms. Then, you have to get comfortable presenting that to a client.

Laying out your terms can make you feel vulnerable. The client then has the chance to criticize openly your rates and/or your rates vis-à-vis your background, samples, professional experience, and other free-lancers. It can rough up your ego to have someone debate the value of your work.

Here are a few little nuggets of negotiating wisdom: If you remember that this is just business, it is easier to bring the negotiating down to hard-core economics. The fee negotiation process and the actual fees themselves are no reflection of your value as a person.

Fee discussions can surface at any time in a new client relationship: during phone conversations before you have even met the client, in a follow-up letter after a meeting, at a courtesy interview meeting where no assignments are being discussed, at a networking luncheon, and even if a prospect is not in the market for free-lancers at all.

Try not to be the first to bring up the subject of payment and fees. It can inject discomfort into any discussions with potential clients, so allow the client to take the initiative. You should do your best to keep the discussion focused at first on the client's needs, your terrific writing samples, and your invaluable service and dependability. But you must be ready to talk money eventually.

If a prospect launches immediately into "what do you charge?" you probably have not had much time to learn about the company's communications budgets, its attitude toward free-lancers, and its flexibility. You are therefore at a disadvantage. The best policy is to try to stall or generalize about your fee structure:

"Well, generally I like to customize my fee approach with all clients. Some of my clients prefer me to work on an hourly basis, including my commuting time, research, etc. But others like to decide a specific charge for each assignment based on a bid. How would you like me to work with you?"

At this point, the client will have to talk about the specific assignment or types of assignments you might be doing and how the company pays free-lancers for these assignments. One way or the other, it refocuses the discussion on the work ahead. Then, when the client turns it back to you, you are armed with more information and can adjust your financial strategy better.

Negotiating Strategies

When you come to verbal negotiations, have in your head your hoped-for fee as well as the bottom dollar you can accept without wounding your pride or your wallet. If you are building a business, however, it can never hurt to compromise your fee expectations. This rule applies no matter how you set your fees.

Some clients already have a set budget per publication, article, brochure, or script and will not leave room for any negotiating. They may not be able to, for reasons that have nothing to do with you. Listen to the client; let him or her tell you if the company has a restricted format or payment approach. The client may say up front, "Listen, we pay five hundred dollars for these columns. Is that all right with you?"

Realize that if you balk, someone else is waiting in the wings to snap up the assignment. It is always possible to say that you are accustomed to earning somewhat more for editorial assignments of that nature, but you want the assignment regardless. Tell the client that you consider it an investment in a future relationship with the company. This kind of response makes it subtly but abundantly clear that this fee is not as much as you would normally charge for such an assignment, and that you hope to get more in the future.

If the client turns the fee question back to you and quizzes you about what you "normally charge," then you have to be ready to recite your fee spiel. My standard approach is to position my negotiating by first telling the client I will work within whatever budget restrictions that client may have. Continue hammering away at the fact that you customize your fee arrangements with all clients, but then use this chance to explain which method, if any, worked out best with other clients.

If you are building a long-term relationship here, then you will want to leave open the possibility of revising your fee arrangement at some later date. You're satisfied for now, but you can even suggest that you discuss this again six months down the road, after the client has seen and likes your work product.

I try to feel out my clients about how they like to work with free-lancers and spin off that experience.

If they say, "Well, we usually pay between five hundred and a thousand dollars for these features," I'll usually take in that information and then restate what my responsibilities for the given assignment will probably be.

For instance, I might reply: "OK, well, in looking at past issues of the magazine, I noticed that writers are generally interviewing only one or two sources. For this article, you've suggested I talk to at least three people—two in person and one on the phone in Europe. And you want two drafts of the article. That suggests to me that I'll probably be toward the higher end of your budget."

This usually prompts the client to want to shut down this discussion quickly, so she or he will chime in with something like this: "Good point. This one will require a few more interviews. OK. How about eight-fifty?"

With a new client, you will not want to extend this negotiation session. It is time to call it a day and shake, when you know there is only another $150 to play with, the article is not the most complex assignment possible, and you are a new writer for this client.

Restating the parameters of the assignment sometimes also refreshes the client's memory about the additional responsibilities they have loaded onto the assignment unknowingly. It also helps define the assignment again for all parties. Here's another example:

"Let me make sure I understand that the brochure will require me to meet with and interview the four top people in marketing in person, as well as read the last ten years' worth of previous brochures for the department. Fine. Then, after I complete the rough draft and you approve the copy, I will be doing the copy approvals with the marketing people. Right? Then, I'll get you a final draft that reflects your changes, as well as their comments and changes. Is that right?"

Perhaps this client forgot about the additional request she or he made, to have you get copy approval from the source: "Oh, did I ask you to call the sources for approvals? That's right. I'll be in Paris and won't be able to do it before production begins. I guess that elevates this brochure to the thousand-dollar category."

If the client has any budget flexibility at all, and really wants you to write the copy, he or she will probably readjust the fee suggestions on the spot. Most people do not like sitting around talking about money or how much a vendor's services are worth. But if you are charging champagne prices for your writing, and they are operating with a beer budget, be ready to compromise your taste if you want this client's business.

The Hourly Versus the Set-Fee Approach

I like working on an hourly basis if I can. It requires more accounting for them and for my own records, but it more accurately reflects what my services are worth in the end. On the other hand, the set-fee basis works to a quick writer's advantage, so I sometimes come out ahead this way after I figure out my hours on a project. One big drawback is that if I have not defined the assignment's parameters vigilantly, I could lose money if the assignment drags on unpredictably.

Setting up an hourly rate can be tricky, however. You do not want to state a high rate that a client will choke on, and at the same time, you do not want to have the client laughing at your underpricing either. The free-lance market these days, in Chicago, runs anywhere from $25/hour to $125/hour, with experienced writers generally falling in the $50 to $75 range.

Specialized writers' fees often exceed this range, and regional differences dictate different scales. For instance, a New York free-lancer can command about 20 percent more than these figures. A Spokane free-lancer must generally *scale back* from the Chicago figures by about 20 percent.

No matter where you live or what your rates are, do not dump an hourly rate on clients too soon. Try to feel out your client early on what might make her or him flinch and be sorry you were ever given an assignment. You will get a quick read by looking at the quality of the publications, the depth of the articles/brochures written, and the frequency of publications. If they are slick, four-color productions with fifteen-hundred- to two-thousand-word articles and many photos inside, you might guess the client is working with a nice budget.

On the other hand, if all they've produced is a one-page, desktop job in two colors or black and white on newsprint-stock paper with a packed news hole and lots of softball team scores, you can guess that they are under tight budget restrictions, no matter how often the publication comes out. Determining this can be difficult and speculative, but it is to your benefit to get a feel for the client's wallet before revealing what you charge.

If, in a given set of negotiations, you think your hourly fee is too rich for a company's blood, scale down. It is easier to state a slightly lower hourly rate early on, than to state a higher set fee that the client may flatly decline. Try to avoid giving prospective clients an hourly rate range, such as: "I charge between fifty-five and a hundred dollars an hour." They might think you are lying about this range, or that some clients do not know they are being cheated.

On the other hand, it cannot hurt to state that you "typically charge sixty-five dollars an hour, depending on the assignment and circumstances."

Sometimes clients may gasp at an hourly rate, which is your cue to explain how you figure your rates, which parts are negotiable, and that you always submit bids. Tell the client up front that in your bid you will clearly outline a specific hour and fee range for a given project. Add that your final charge will not exceed the bid range unless the client expands the responsibilities of the assignment midway.

Make it clear to a client, especially a new one, that you always send a follow-up confirmation letter that restates the project responsibilities and your anticipated compensation. This should allay the fears of many clients who may hesitate working with someone who has "the meter running."

On-the-Spot Bids

At some point you may have to bid against other free-lancers for a given project, or a client may want you to complete this step even if you are the only person being considered. If this happens, I recommend the following approach. First tell the client you always send clients a follow-up letter confirming any assignment's parameters and expected fees. (For a bid letter sample, see Chapter VII, "Follow Up in Style.")

If you are dealing with the client in person when he or she asks for the bid, try to outline the bid on the spot. Sometimes that can be tough, because you do not want to commit to an unfavorable financial arrangement. At the same time, it gives you the opportunity to educate the client—about all the technical specifics involved in this job, what is involved in doing any corporate communications assignments, and the lengths to which you will go in pleasing clients and doing a good job.

The basics of the bid, spoken and written, should include a narrative explanation of what you will be doing on the assignment, before you state a dollar figure. For instance, you might describe the number of interviews, overseas phone calls, car or plane trips, lunches, on-site tours, library research, outlining, number of drafts, and so on. After that, you can write a chronological listing of those responsibilities, along with how much time you expect to need to complete them.

That time estimate should be a range of times, with the total fee range calculated at the end. Try the following format:

SAMPLE ESTIMATE

Action	Estimated Time
On-site interview, with marketing manager	.75–1.25 hours
Two phone interviews with operations people	1.50–2.75 hours
Corporate library research	1.25–1.75 hours
Outline	.75–1.50 hours
Draft 1	4.50–5.75 hours
Draft 2	1.75–3.50 hours
TOTAL TIME	10.50–16.50 hours
TOTAL CHARGE	$ –

Awaiting the Verdict

After you've packaged up the bid with a cover letter on your stationery, prepare to wait for the client's decision. If the client is producing the communications assignment in a hurry, then you'll hear soon. If not, and it's a major project, it may be weeks before you hear.

More than once I've burned the midnight oil to crank out lengthy proposals with projected hours and fees for huge projects. Then, the prospective client who'd required the proposal in a hurry didn't respond for seven months. That's a lot of work with no compensation in sight, but it comes with the free-lance territory.

Other clients ask for the bids on the fly but respond immediately. I once faxed a bid to a client who quickly called me up to open the negotiations. We chatted more about the project, its parameters, and then I gave up a little here, a little there. In exchange, I asked for more latitude on the interviewing threshold than he originally wanted to hold me to. He agreed. So although we pinched my fees at one end, we agreed to scale back certain responsibilities. He faxed back his scratched-up bid, and I put together a final, clean bid with the changes.

As your confidence and experience grow, you will learn to stand by your bids and not back down in any major ways. I find that if a client balks at a bid completely, it's time to go through it item by item and talk about each part of the project and the amount of time needed to complete it.

Most clients will understand and appreciate your finagling, if you're logical and straightforward.

Working on "Spec"

I have occasionally run across a new-business situation where the client prospect asks me to write something without being guaranteed any payment or only partial payment. This isn't any effort to cheat me out of my appropriate compensation. In exchange, the client guarantees me a specific piece of business when it becomes a reality. However, knowing the assignment is on "spec," or *on speculation*, I make sure we both understand what my responsibilities and compensation, if any, will be in the end.

After some discussion about the situation's parameters, I usually agree to do it, especially knowing that I can expect more business or the rest of the writing assignment. Typically, these situations arise for these reasons:

- The client wants to see a sample of my writing before assigning me to a project.
- I'm subcontracting to a client who still hasn't received *his or her* client's go-ahead for a project; but my client still needs my writing samples for a presentation or bid.

- My client considers an agreed-on partial payment as a "kill fee," in case the project never happens.
- The client wants me to write the proposal for a project, with the understanding that I will be the eventual writer for it when it is approved and funded.

Checking Up on Invoices

Generally, my clients pay me within fifteen to thirty days. Before I launch any project, with a new client particularly, I like to iron out this kind of detail when we've almost wrapped up a deal. You can discuss it rather informally, but you'd better find out for sure.

I've been surprised by some rather lengthy waits for payment, either because I didn't ask what the accounts payable cycle was, or I didn't request a specific pay period. This shunted me into a long-term, sometimes forty-five- to sixty-day cycle. That can really disturb a free-lancer's cash flow.

Once I establish a working relationship with a client and have cashed a few checks from them, these procedures usually happen without a hitch. Once in a while, I experience an unexplained delay. In these situations I wait until a couple days after I should have received the check and then call the client. The client usually has to check up on the Accounting department and see where the check was held up in the process. Other times, I've learned later that my invoice never traveled beyond my client's desk. Now, that's disturbing.

Anyway, you have every right to inquire about your invoice payment schedule. Just don't do it prematurely or you'll look pitifully desperate for cash, which doesn't sound appropriate for a successful free-lancer.

On other (hopefully rare) occasions, you might actually run into a client who says the company won't pay you because your work was inadequate. Then you do have a problem. If you're on the phone with the client when you hear this, ask her or him to explain. Then tell the client you'll call back after digging up your file and invoice. Don't apologize and don't argue with the client at this point, even if you think you fulfilled your responsibilities adequately.

Once off the phone, you must review all your work files from the project as well as your invoice. Make sure you added up your hours correctly (if you were on an hourly rate) or that you billed for the agreed-upon set fee. Then, look back at your original bid or agreement with the client, from before you ever began the work. Compare this with the final work product you gave the client. Ask yourself some objective questions:

- Did you deliver the work on time?
- Did you follow the client's specific directions on what subjects should be covered?
- Did you organize it according to the client's directions?
- Did you conform to the company's style or creative standards?
- Was the writing too long? too short? too verbose? too florid?
- Did you overlook many typos?
- Did you misquote or misrepresent someone's background comments?

Consider all these kinds of questions as you look through your final work product. Then decide whether you did what the client asked and call him or her back to talk further. Perhaps, if your work passed your scrupulous standards, some other issue is coming into play. Maybe the client has a new boss who decided he or she didn't like your work. Try and find out.

Unfortunately, most of a free-lance writer's deals will be made without any legal contract backing them up. The only evidence you really have of any agreement will be your follow-up letters. (This gives you yet another incentive to maintain rigorous follow-up procedures after any client interaction!) Refer to any bid letters to your client, without being antagonistic if possible. Explain how you understood you were to undertake the project and how you would be compensated.

Although I have never been in this situation, I imagine that if a client dispute ever reached such a confrontational level and I presented substantial proof of my fulfilling my end of the bargain, the client would back off somehow and cough up part if not the whole amount of the invoice.

Such a problem could certainly dampen, if not terminate, a relationship with any client. (More about losing a client in Chapter XIII, "Revitalize Your Business.")

Chapter IX

Now That You're the Hired Gun

ALTHOUGH YOU MAY feel the war is won once you've landed an assignment, more work lies ahead. Keep in mind that a corporate communications free-lancer needs to put into play many of the same skills as a consumer journalist. In other words, you need to be not only a good writer, but a keen observer and listener, and an organized thinker as well. These skills surface when you actually pursue your topics, information, and interviews. On top of that, you will also be required to follow the rules of each corporation, which means acting like an insider right from the start. This is "public relations" after all.

If you're new to a client company, and you've followed the client-targeting suggestions in Chapter V, you've already gathered the basic background you need to understand what the company is all about—its products and services as well as the context in which any given assignment fits.

In addition, you should ask to see the company orientation video, a corporate organization chart, the annual report, recent back issues of the company newsletter or marketing magazine, and product or identity brochures, before tackling any initial assignments. You may not have had access to these kinds of communications before you became an insider. Now they'll serve to illuminate you on several issues:

- Who your client likes to use for primary sources in communications

- Whether the company relies solely on upper management for background
- How candid the inside sources are allowed to be in interviews
- How much the company goes to outside resources for communications
- How much freedom the company allows in design, writing style, general creativity, and rank-and-file input
- How big the publication/communications budgets are

Researching an Assignment

Perhaps the biggest differences between consumer journalism and corporate communications will surface during the researching and interviewing of background sources for assignments. Confidentiality and trade competition influence this environment more than anything. No company wants its product/service secrets released prematurely, for fear that the competition might grab them for their own or begin simultaneous development of a similar or derivative product.

Consumer business journalists are typically funneled into the Media Relations department, to control what information is quoted and to keep unfortunate off-the-cuff comments from being printed. Even after they've developed relationships with internal people, the journalists may still be shunted back to Media Relations, which will determine the safest way to position some issue or concept. Many companies school their employees in the art of dealing with journalists and the need to refer them to Media Relations.

A constant refrain I hear among corporate people who are thrown to the media "wolves" is that they were misquoted or taken out of context. In the safe bosom of their corporate family, of which you are now a part, they should never fear these alleged journalistic indiscretions. With all the editing, proofing, and courtesy reviews granted to sources for internally produced publications, undesirable words or sentiments should never make it to final copy.

Corporate communications clients will not want to leave anything to chance when they have free-lancers come in to complete an assignment. The client often bends over backward to make sure the writer receives "correct" information from a controlled stack of background materials and will carefully choose a politically sensitive and diverse set of interview sources for additional information.

This simplifies the free-lancer's job in many ways and ensures the right slant on a subject. Even if the sources do not offer appropriate, approved opinions, their comments will be sanitized or perked up during the approval and proofing process.

So what's the same about this and journalism? Well, the client controls the information dished out to both contract writers and consumer/trade journalists. But that same in-house communicator can't control the amount of digging a consumer journalist will do to confirm or uncover some information from beyond the palace walls.

Interviewing Corporate Sources

In order to complete many corporate assignments, a writer will have to interview in-house sources for background, history, research materials, and general industry information. Some corporations have clear standards and procedures for how these interviews are conducted; others leave writers to their own devices.

If you are writing about a new product or breakthrough service, then you must dig out all the facts/issues/challenges from a key person or team involved with the project. These interviews provide the primary information to substantiate a piece, because no published information may be available on the topic, even through the library.

For instance, I was involved with writing several different

communications pieces for a company that was experimenting with and synthesizing fat-replacement ingredients, years before fat-replaced products gripped our grocery-aisle consciousness. It was an unprecedented situation, and I had to bone up on some specific chemical compositions and interactions and then sort out with my internal source how these new ingredients might be adapted for food applications. Even the scientist was still speculating about these opportunities, because he had originally formulated the ingredient for a completely different purpose.

That was an unusual backgrounding situation that evolved as the assignment took shape. My primary client at that company basically gave me my entrée to the internal source, reminded me of the strict confidentiality of this product development, and then let me loose.

Some Will Help, Others Will Hinder

Some companies have specific protocol set up for outside writers conducting research. Maybe they won't have you write about a certain product because you wrote for its competition once before. Some may have you stay on the outside for all backgrounding, and they'll discreetly parcel out pieces of information as they see fit, rather than letting you off the leash within the corporate walls.

Some corporate clients will hand me what I fondly call a "prefab story." All I have to do is put the nuts and bolts in the right places, according to the instructions. This little package might include a stack of background materials, promotion brochures, annual reports, a corporate phone directory complete with little Post-its signaling the specific interviewees, and an outline of how the client anticipates the assignment will be organized. Then the client might stick you in an office down the hall to polish off the assignment in record time, under his or her nose, and play computer "editing tag" later in the day.

On the other hand, another corporate client might have absolutely no printed information at all to give you on a specific subject, and leave you to your own devices in tracking down background material. This is when most writers need to dig out facts and work with internal sources before any writing can begin. Sometimes these clients just call you with a list of people and phone numbers and say, "Go for it."

Some in-person interview situations will be more formal than others, some may happen over lunch, still others might occur on the fly while the person works on some rig. Or you may find yourself conducting scores of interviews on the phone. One way or the other, there are many murky dos and don'ts involved in interviewing internal corporate sources.

Some of those gray areas include:

- Establishing contact with internal sources
- Working with gatekeepers (receptionists, secretaries)
- Establishing rapport with sources
- Looking for clues about your sources
- Tape recording
- Conducting interviews with your client present
- Establishing telephone interview etiquette
- Making international calls
- Acting in the company's interests
- Handling difficult ethical situations

Contacting sources can sometimes present its own curious set of problems. Even if you have the go-ahead to call your sources, find out if your client pre-interviewed or at least alerted the source about your phone call and eventual interview. This solves any awkwardness that might ensue as the source tries to understand who you are and whether you truly have the blessing of the Communications department to be doing what you're doing. Try to avoid this kind of conflict, as it can negatively color all your dealings with that source.

You may also find that before you finally set up a specific time and place for the interview, you have to make several inquiries with gatekeepers. (More about handling gatekeepers in Chapter VI, "Navigate the Marketing Maze.") If your primary client hasn't done so for you already, just explain who you are to a secretary or receptionist who is trying to protect the boss from unnecessary distractions. Most gatekeepers are extremely helpful, especially if the boss isn't exactly a corporate celebrity and doesn't get a lot of ink in corporate publications.

If the source is teetering toward the top rung of a corporate ladder, then she or he may not be so enthusiastic about *another* interview. You may need to ask your client to intervene and light a fire under the source's Bunsen burner to elicit some cooperation.

In the event that you and the source continue playing phone tag with each other's voice mail, then by all means specify several days and time blocks when you can be available for an interview. Tell him or her through voice mail merely to call back and leave another message confirming the most convenient time option.

It also can't hurt to fax or voice-mail a list of some general subject areas you plan to cover. I have on occasion worked with sources who not only demanded this, but also edited the questions or outline even before I'd ever interviewed them.

After a brief conversation to set up an interview, one corporate source asked me to fax the questions and an outline ahead of time. Then he edited these both to his satisfaction, faxed them back, and asked to see a corrected copy. Wow! Only then was he ready to set up an interview time. I mentioned this to my client, who admitted this sometimes happens. (The client, however, emphasized that I shouldn't fail to charge for this extra work.)

In the Flesh

Once you have set up an in-person interview time, then you have to deal with some new variables and establish a rapport with the source. What will this person be like? Will this source open up easily and give you the information you need? Will you have to pull the information from him or her? Will the source be articulate? When you show up, you'll find out quickly how the time will be spent.

Before you go, think about how you'll dress for the occasion. For instance, if you have to interview a transport driver at a remote rural location, business attire might make your source uncomfortable and lead to a wooden interview. On the other hand, slumping into a chair in the chief financial officer's office in a sweater and slacks might be interpreted as disrespectful.

In order to elicit the best information and the most candid responses from any subject, you need to adapt quickly to the immediate environment and make the subject comfortable. A flexible attitude and appropriate dress go a long way to showing a subject that you respect his or her workplace, the rigors of the work at hand, and the information to be offered you.

Try to get to the interview five to ten minutes early. Shake hands with the source firmly and enthusiastically. If the source offers you a beverage, take one if you're thirsty. Don't be shy; he or she is trying to help *you* relax, too. Appreciate the gesture.

Once you're in the source's office, look around for clues that tell you about this person and how he or she works. Get a visual feel for what this person is like and what she or he does on a daily basis. Pictures from the family ski trip? Any finger paintings by children? Or is there an eighteen-wheeler replica poised at the edge of the desk? Evidence of cigarettes? A Nerf basketball hoop in the room? Two computers? An artist's drawing table? Three dead plants? Running shoes and cross-country skis stuck in the corner? A bubble gum machine that requires pennies? Lots of awards, plaques, and trophies?

All kinds of clues help set you up for the interview before you even ask the first question. As you're observing the source settling down for the interview, it's time to establish some relationship with him or her. This is a necessary, albeit superficial, rapport you must develop if you want to elicit the best information possible under the circumstances.

Ask some preliminary questions that allow sources to relax and talk about themselves. It helps them organize their thoughts and warm up to articulating coherently about their products or services, their ambitions for the company, their strategy-building techniques, their own contributions. This preliminary conversation may not end up in your written product, but it will help you put this person in a context while they practice shaping their opinions.

At the same time, the source may ask you about you: how you've hooked up with the company and what got you started free-lancing. (Don't necessarily tell all, if it means saying you hate having a boss or working for any rigidly structured company.)

Yes, this pre-interview chitchat might be labeled frivolous "sharing time," but I find it helps me predict just how the forthcoming interview will proceed. I also like to chalk up these chats to relationship building. It's something I like to do whether or not it has any immediate value. I'm not embarrassed to say I indulge in it on many occasions.

Next you'll want to segue into a brief rundown of the information you're looking for and how you expect to conduct the interview. This means explaining in your own words what you understand about the project or subject, and then outlining the types of questions you'll be asking.

At the same time, get approval before taping an interview, if you plan to record it for later transcription or reference. This is a good idea if the information is highly technical or if you want the source to feel comfortable that you won't butcher the concept when you try to regurgitate his or her comments later. Just make sure you ask permission from the source and explain why it's necessary to tape this particular interview. If the source denies your request to tape, then put the darn recorder away.

You will conduct yourself pretty much the same way if your primary communications client attends the interview as well. Subtly find out ahead of time what the client's objectives are for attending it. Is the client curious about the subject and trying to bone up on it? Is the client reluctant to let you off the leash in the corporate office for security reasons or because you might commit some public relations gaffe? Or is this just a sensitive interviewee who needs to be handled with public relations' finest doeskin gloves?

Depending on how well you know the client, this may or may not be distracting as you formulate questions or establish rapport with a source. Your client may know the source and subject quite well, which could put you in the position of unwittingly asking some redundant questions. Or, if the client is unfamiliar with the subject and source, he or she may end up essentially conducting the interview without your getting in a word edgewise. If you have your questions prepared ahead of time, you won't flounder in any case. And if the client does monopolize the interview, great! You'll find out exactly what direction your client wants you to go in for the written piece.

On the Phone

You can also gather information by interviewing sources over the telephone, depending on your client's requirements. However, these interviews still call for a certain amount of etiquette.

If a client approves this type of interview and gives you the go-ahead, then set up the interview time as formally as you would an in-person discussion. Oftentimes sources will want to know specifically how long the phone interview will take. Although that's hard to predict, try to stay within a thirty-minute time frame. The source may balk at anything longer than that.

Take into account any time zone differences, crank up your personal computer or notepad, and start taking notes when you hook up with the interviewee. It's somewhat harder to establish relationships with people via phone, but launch the interview with the same kind of personal/professional questions you would ask at any in-person interview: how long has the interviewee worked at the company, where did she or he come from, academic credentials, motivations for new projects, and so on.

When conducting phone interviews, decide whether you'll do it over a speaker phone, through a headset, or by crooking the phone under your chin. Some sources may not like to know that their voices are being broadcast over a speaker phone, even if they understand you're at a home office.

Also, remember that any extraneous noises (clicking computer keys, dogs barking, other people talking) will be heard at the same time. Holding the phone between your shoulder and head will only give you a stiff neck and a chiropractor's bill. Try using a headset. They're inexpensive and more cost-effective than buying yourself a worker's compensation policy, and they work.

International calls for interviews pose other challenges. Language barriers, time zones, and different business customs each play a role in making your international interviews work or not. Staying up until midnight to call Turkey, and then having to leave a message for a callback from a source, can deteriorate your good humor and expand your sleep deficit.

And if you're juggling calls to several different countries, be strategic and know yourself. If you're the kind of person who doesn't mind pulling an all-nighter once in a while, then book all the calls for one night. If you prefer to dilute the pain, then book only one per night.

When you do attempt to make contact at some remote locations around the world, remember that some country's phone systems might be characterized as quaint or old-fashioned. This means trouble. It's hard enough to conduct interviews over the phone, much less when the connection is weak, you're both attempting to speak English, and the interviewee is speaking with a heavy accent.

A Fragile Balance

Corporate interviews can frustrate free-lancers who come from a journalism background. You're digging up good information, but you want more. You're hunting not just for the dirt but for the truffles as well. So you restrain yourself to avoid any controversy or you'll be tossed out onto the street.

Writing for corporations means you're putting out high-quality publications or communications that present the facts in the most appropriate, flattering light. You've been chosen to act in the *company's best interests,* so realize that this is public relations, not investigative journalism. If you have trouble reconciling yourself to this, then consider looking at it this way: You're dressing the meat of the story with a delicious sauce.

Ask provocative questions during interviews and use some of that information, wisely. It will all go through an approval process of some sort anyway. Just be sure not to provoke your client by revealing the company's dirty laundry in your writing. It wouldn't be good for your business.

I talk about this PR/journalistic balance somewhat glibly. That's because I have never run into a situation where my personal or professional integrity was at stake. I'm lucky. Some writers do run into marginally unethical situations and don't know what to do.

Say, for instance, that in the process of writing some corporate publication you stumbled over the fact that the company was knowingly dumping a toxic substance illegally. Without hesitation I would explain to my internal client what I knew and how this affected my ability to work for the company. I would probably quit the assignment, yes, even before I'd billed them or received payment. I would proceed the same way in most any other ethics conflict. Put the onus on the client to give you direction on how to deal with a situation. Then, if you can't live with that, politely sever your relationship. Fortunately these occasions rarely come up.

The Corporate Library

Some companies will allow you to conduct thorough research through their internal corporate library, which may have access to some extensive legal and business information databases. Sometimes these arrangements are made under the supervision of a librarian or communications person. Sometimes the writer is allowed to wander the halls and peruse the corporate library stacks independently.

As part of their internal library, some companies will maintain archives that collect corporate memorabilia and historical documents dating back to the company's start-up. If you're allowed access to these mementos for background, you are being allowed a rare glimpse into how the company evolved, and how customers' and consumers' tastes became what they are today.

Although background from interviews and the corporate library may fill gaps in information, it can never hurt a writer to conduct outside research on a given topic at a public library. Tell your client you're doing this, before launching into outside research. Then quiz the reference librarian and hunt through the computerized periodical listings for anything remotely touching on the subject you're addressing. Your client will likely appreciate the additional elbow grease and interest.

Deadline Dilemmas

Completing and then delivering assignments to clients on time can provoke anxiety in some of the most seasoned free-lancers. If you're a procrastinator, you probably experience heart palpitations just thinking about deadlines.

While most corporate communicators deal with copy and production deadlines, they generally aren't handcuffed to a newspaper-style daily production cycle that happens whether the copy's there or not. Mostly they're working with "elastic" deadlines, only you aren't supposed to know that.

Corporate communicators compose "back-timed" production schedules for corporate publications and productions, by working backward on the calendar from the project's expected distribution date. With that actual distribution or presentation date, the in-house communicator then consults production staff and outside consultants to determine how long it will take to print a publication or final-edit an A/V project. He or she builds into that a buffer zone of days, for slow distribution, reworking, or errors, for example.

Then, the communicator figures out how many days or weeks it will take to pull together the design elements, field production, writing, and photography. This is an amorphous period of time when most communicators attempt to complete all these steps simultaneously. This doesn't always work. Many times the photography and field production play off the copy, which is why the writers are usually contacted first and asked to complete their end of the project pronto.

This is how the "absolute" versus "elastic" deadline came into being. The communicator may call with an assignment and a deadline, but may still have to cement the assignment's content and objectives. So, you have an assignment and you know when it needs to be finished, but you can't start on it right away if you don't have the interviewee names and a basic idea of what you're supposed to be writing about. That's when the communicator generously offers you a few extra days to finish the job, "if you need it."

Although this scenario can happen, it's best to stick with a hard-and-fast personal rule to get assignments in when clients ask for them, with or without the quotes if necessary. That way, your professional credibility and integrity stay intact.

Writing Tone and Approach

By the time you've finished gathering data, you should have a good idea what writing style and tone appeals to your client. You've reviewed back issues of publications or videos. You've taken notes and have a knowledge of some of the style elements this company and client prefer to see in their publications or communications.

These style elements might be common to any communications, whether they're directed toward a consumer or internal corporate audience. Many companies choose to use a straight, news-style approach and follow a guide like *The Associated Press Stylebook* on many elements. For other elements, such as quotes or descriptive approach, in-house communicators may defer to what the company's management prefers.

These style elements might include:

- Lots of quotes or sound bites (for A/V) from rank and file
- No quotes in leads
- Few quotes, if any, in articles or brochures
- Liberal use of analogies, similes
- People referred to by first (or last) names in articles
- Colorful descriptions of people, places, things
- Short (or long) paragraphs, short (or long) sentences
- Company hierarchy involvement played down (or up)
- Yes (or no) to subheads

Packaging Up That Final Product

When you're ready to ship off that final piece of writing to meet the deadline, you need to review some specifics. Is it printed and packaged according to the client's specifications? Make sure you find out well in advance how each client likes to receive assignments. While some won't care what the document looks like as long as they receive some kind of hard copy, others have specific requirements you need to find out about. Consider asking about and checking on the following items:

- Line spacing and margins for an article/script
- Print style (dot matrix/laser/ink jet) or manual typewriter
- Typeface
- Hard copy and/or diskette
- Will you need to convert to another word processing application?
- Does the client want a perfect first draft, or is a rewrite built into your assignment responsibilities?

Delivering the Assignment?

These days there are many ways you can get a document to a client. If the company is fairly nearby, you have your pick of messengers, overnight express services, the U.S. mail, or dropping it off yourself. Then there are the electronic ways to send a document: modems, facsimile machines, electronic mail services like CompuServe or Prodigy.

It's up to you to find out what clients prefer. Some may not like the idea that documents containing trade secrets will be unprotected as they zip over some electronic mail system. Some may prefer to receive a paper copy and a diskette. Others may say they don't want to pay for messengers or overnight services, so you'll either have to eat that cost, build in extra days for mailing time, or make the trip yourself.

Fulfilling these simple requirements of a client will help you ingratiate yourself to her or him. Become indispensable by making the client's job easier. Don't make the client do any extra work to bring your document, or your writing, up to his or her company and individual standards.

Computing Your Bill

I relish this last step in any client project: calculating and sending out an invoice. Once I'm finished with a project, per the client's specifications, I tally up the hours I've spent on the project. I do this even if I gave the client a flat-rate bid. It helps me know if I spent my work time efficiently and if I need to rethink my approach to bidding in the future.

I follow a standard billing format for my work, but there are myriad ways to put bills together. Generally, I use a memo style for the basic information. Then I tick off the services I rendered, and within what period of time I did so. At the end of the line, in the right margin, I write the dollar total, which is based on my hourly rate or a fixed fee. Here's an example:

INVOICE

TO: Mr. Pal Client
        Blind Faith Corporation

FROM: Maryclaire Collins
        COLLINS Communications

DATE: March 1, 1994

RE: Editorial consulting services rendered on the
        corporate orientation video, at a rate of
        $—— per hour.

Services rendered from 1/14/94 to 2/28/94, including:

Three on-site meetings;
two telephone interviews with sources;
researching at corporate library and archives;
reviewing published materials and videos;
first draft and one rewrite;
attending one production session;
coordinating and attending one editing session.

38.75 total hours
total due $____

Please forward payment within 15 working days to:

Maryclaire Collins
COLLINS Communications
Address

SS#_____
Invoice #_____

Once you have finished the bill, check your hours again and re-tally the dollars. You'd be surprised how many errors can surface when you don't check and recheck your numbers.

Chapter X

Free-lance Writer as Art Director

CLIENTS SOMETIMES SOLICIT a free-lance writer's input on the design or production of a print piece or A/V project. You need to decide whether you can legitimately jump into this side of a project, if you should bail out, or if you should take some life-saving courses in production or design.

Understand that even a smattering of production knowledge will help you appreciate and follow the production cycle. This dilettante's background will also give you perspective on how you fit into the assignment's total picture and how so many other people's work product depends on how well you fulfill your writing responsibilities.

Cultivate a Graphic Eye

Regardless of whether you're ever called on to contribute anything to the design or production of a communications effort, you need to develop your eye for what looks good on paper or on screen. You also need to understand why a certain image, graphic, or photograph is used or is better than another.

What images best convey a specific message? How do design and layout forward the objectives of a publication and each specific article? How does a photograph complement copy? What else does an image communicate? How can a photo or graphic distract from the copy's message? How do you humanize a buttoned-down corporate situation in photographs?

Even if you are fulfilling only the written part of a project, it's good to have some impression of what the client expects the finished product to look like. If nothing else, it will give you an idea of how your client's eye works and what graphic, design, or other visual images he or she prefers.

For print products, perhaps he or she likes open designs with lots of white space and large, stark graphics and illustrations. For an A/V project, maybe the client travels the computer-generated graphics route only. Maybe your client is experimenting with more news-style video productions.

This information all adds to your background when dealing with the client in general. As you're gathering this information, your mission should be to learn as much as you can about how your client expedites print and audiovisual production.

The two processes turn up hundreds of variables that must be handled and coordinated. These are just a sample of the questions clients and I mull over in the process of completing a communications project:

- How complicated is it to produce certain photos or on-screen images?
- What are the pros and cons of black-and-white versus color print production?
- At what point does it become too expensive to make changes in the print production process?
- How sophisticated must a desktop publishing system be to save the client money?
- Why should a client go with one paper stock over another?
- Do photos reproduce better on a coated paper stock?
- When does a layout distract from the messages being conveyed?
- If a client can't afford photography, can other graphic images, like snappy call-outs or captions, effectively break up the page?

- How do you know which typeface and point size will work better with different communications pieces?
- Will a client save money or help the environment by using recycled paper stocks?
- Is it cheaper and more effective to produce an interactive computer disk for people instead of a video?

Keep in mind that technological advances continually change the print and A/V production processes. This means that you particularly need to stay on top of what's happening in production technology. It enhances your value to clients if you can assist them in the myriad choices available.

The Print Side

Having some print production experience, preferably hands-on, really adds to a free-lancer's skills repertoire. Even if you don't actually produce the finished publications for a client, you must be able to roughly sketch, envision, or explain some design concepts or elements. You should also be able to converse intelligently about layouts and design to help some clients visualize a final product.

Some clients will have sophisticated, on-site production facilities and production coordinators who handle everything. The only outside vendor they may use is the printer. Others may contract outside vendors for each step of the process. Others might not have the foggiest notion of how to begin the process. This is where your production background can come in handy.

If you have absolutely no knowledge of this area of communications, don't fake it with these clients. Instead, get yourself to one of the many production workshops offered by professional communicators' associations in most metropolitan areas. (Look in Chapter XII, "The Networking Necessity," for a list of associations.)

However, if you do have some facility with production, play up your expertise to less knowledgeable and needy clients. You might even consider adding some graphics software to your personal computing environment at home.

Some free-lance writers make tidy additional profits by offering desktop publishing services simultaneously with their writing services. At this juncture you need to consider how much of your practice you want to devote to desktop publishing. Then you have to weigh whether that or writing is your true love and talent. It is a rare combination to be a really good writer *and* a really good layout/design artist.

Short of becoming a desktop publisher and corporate writer, you can offer your services as a "production coordinator" for projects. Sometimes I have found myself dumped into the role by default; other times I have engineered the position for myself. That way, I can charge for coordination time in addition to writing time.

One way or the other, any print product goes through several stages before it's finally distributed, as previously discussed. And generally the client coordinates photography and reviews designs, layouts, copy approvals, and paper stock options. Then print production can begin in earnest.

"Once you have the copy and design concepts approved, you have to marry the two," says Pamela Lyons, sales communication manager and former production editor at the CNA Insurance Companies. "With desktop publishing, designers lay out copy via software programs like Pagemaker and QuarkXPress. Once a designer imports the text file, he or she will access the software program's graphic applications in order to spec type. This means the designer is choosing typefaces and point sizes for headlines, subheads, body copy, call-out quotes, etc., as well as making good use of white space (leading). In conjunction with this task, they also position any supporting graphics such as illustrations and photos."

The designers then begin finessing the layout, when they look for problems such as bad widows and line breaks that inhibit readability. Then they present a desktop "comp" or composition to the in-house client for comments.

Lyons elaborates that every company and Communications department will do things a little differently, but CNA's process for many print communications involves these steps.

A designer might also scan or import original photos and illustrations into the desktop system through scanner peripherals that feed into the computer. He or she can then size them to fit an allotted space in the print piece being produced.

With an in-house desktop system, companies can make changes inexpensively during the review process, instead of turning the piece back to an outside designer to be laid out again. With those changes quickly and simply keyed into a personal computer, the production coordinator can obtain final approvals on the piece.

The second stage of the print production process becomes more involved, when the layouts are produced as camera-ready art-boards and then sent to the printer. At that point the printer shoots photos of each page of the artwork, which includes the text, graphics, and illustrations.

The black-and-white graphics are reproduced in halftones, or the percentages of black and white represented in each photo image. Color graphics are reproduced on four separate sheets of clear film or transparencies. Each transparency page represents one of the four process colors of cyan, yellow, magenta, and black, and the percentages of each used in that particular graphic.

When the printing vendor completes this step, he or she will then give the company a "blueline" or "silverprint" for a two-color or one-color job. If it's a four-color job, the client will receive a "chromalin" to review and approve. All of these are pre-press samples of what the end-product will look like. This is when the client or company can observe if the colors are true to what they expected the piece to look like.

"The dollars start mounting if you make changes at this stage, because the printer has conducted a lot of pre-press, behind-the-scenes preparations in order to make the film that produces the bluelines," says Lyons, a fourteen-year CNA veteran.

"These days a lot of companies don't even produce camera-ready art anymore; they just give the printer a disk with the electronically designed job on it. Some companies and ad agencies are even modeming the electronic file to the printer."

Throughout this process, a writer might have worked with several different people besides his or her primary client. Some of them might have come from outside the client's actual company. A designer, photographer, printer, production coordinator, and copy editor might work on a print piece.

With this kind of staff involved in a project, the writer might not be involved at all once the client is satisfied with the writing. Or the client may call in the writer to review typeset proof sheets and proofread the copy.

The Audiovisual Side

If you have been assigned to write a video script for a client, then you probably have some understanding of how to synchronize the layers of media and sensory elements to be juggled within a script. If you don't, then the first thing you need to learn is a basic script-writing format. You will write the script in two columns, with visual elements on the left and corresponding audio cues on the right side.

Both the audio and video may be multilayered, with several different kinds of visual and auditory elements.

On the audio side, the writer might have to write and integrate music, narration, sound effects, voice-over narration, on-camera narration, natural or ambient sound, and prerecorded sound bites from other sources. Building these into the script is one thing, but merging them seamlessly is quite another.

The writer's job is to incorporate all these audio elements so they do not jar the viewer/listener and distract from the message that needs to be communicated. This requires the use of smooth segues or transitions, gentle fades or sharp cuts, and subtle background noise.

Here are some visual elements you might integrate into an A/V script:

- *Information graphics,* which might outline a process or describe features of a product or service while a narrator elaborates on a voice-over.
- *Illustrative graphics,* which could be artwork or other complementary illustrations for the narrator or music.
- *Computer-generated graphics, titles, and captions,* for people's names, companies, dates, quotes, etc.
- *Lighting cues,* particularly for in-studio shoots that have on-camera talent or panelists or other action
- *Video transitions/dissolves/superimpositions,* to give producer/director a clear idea of how abruptly or subtly the video shots and segments will switch or work with other video.
- *"A" roll video versus "B" roll* might be the main videotaped segments or the scenic, descriptive shots, or cutaway shots that cover jump cuts (or switches) from one shot to another.
- *Prerecorded, dropped-in segments,* typically field-produced video segments that are brought to an editing booth for in-studio mixing of all elements.

You're the Producer Now

If you do have significant audiovisual production experience, then capitalize on it. Do not overlook the opportunities and advantages of being the art director or production supervisor for a project. You can relieve your client of some big headaches if he or she can consolidate several responsibilities with you—the dependable writing vendor.

Even if you aren't currently producing scripts for a given client, look for an opportunity to discuss your experience in this area. Sometimes just mentioning this can jog a client's thinking and jolt her or him into starting on a shelved or new project. The client may respect your audiovisual sensitivity sufficiently that he or she will call you in to observe production and offer input.

My first job out of college was as a production assistant and eventually a producer at a small Chicago television station and production house. During those three years, I had the luck to do a lot of hands-on videotape editing, total production coordination, field production, and script-writing. My boss and longtime mentor encouraged me to jump into any opportunity I could. That experience boosted my confidence, proving to me that I could match up to every new production and writing challenge.

That was the early 1980s. If I had to start now as a writing professional looking for chances to learn A/V production, I'd investigate continuing education seminars and workshops through professional associations or local colleges. And, depending on the market I lived in, I would also look for a part-time internship at a local TV station or production house. Although these positions are highly sought after, it's worth the effort to try to land one.

Chapter XI

Nurturing Your Client Relationships

In ESTABLISHING A NEW client relationship, you will probably conduct yourself somewhat differently from the way you will after several years of working for that client. Maybe you like to deal with clients a little more formally at first, until you've both warmed up to each other.

Perhaps that means a typically exuberant, extroverted type will lay back a bit, listen more, and let the client take the lead more often. Then, after several assignments, you might feel more comfortable and allow your personality to seep into dealings with the client. For another writer, the beginning of a client relationship may require a bit more aggressive interaction, in order to establish a flow of assignments, a predictable rapport, and routine operating procedures.

The ease of a client relationship usually depends on both personalities and how they conflict or mesh. One client may ignore a free-lancer's quirky behavior if his or her writing more than fits the bill. Another client may find those idiosyncrasies so annoying or distracting that they eclipse the writing's brilliance. Rather than try too hard to psych out each client situation and each client's personality, just use common sense when dealing with different kinds of people.

And, mostly, just be yourself. It's too stressful and unproductive to hide your true personality for long, and you have to make the relationships flow as easily as possible if you want to pull in a decent income from repeat client business.

This section will analyze how you can collaborate with your clients at all different stages of your professional relationship to keep your business successful.

Who's Calling the Shots?

At the beginning, it's easier to accept a client's every order and whim, regardless of what you're being paid. Then, after a while you might find yourself debating the merits of various orders. You probably won't mention any of this speculation to the client, but you will think about the situation and measure how you feel about it.

Generally, such orders won't jeopardize your journalistic or ethical integrity, put your ego on the line, or require you to confront the client—unless you know the client is doing something wrong, and that something is putting a wedge into your relationship or compromising your ability to write well. Then you have to grapple with the decision to confront the client.

That "something" can be as simple as a blatant but consistent punctuation violation. Or it could be as profoundly destructive as plagiarism or sexual harassment.

Whatever it is, if it bothers you to the point of distraction, figure out how to discuss it diplomatically with the client. But before you do that, try to predict how the client will react, and decide if the situation is important enough to risk losing a client. Maybe a style error isn't an earth-shattering-enough problem to risk your business, and forcing the issue would only label you as a grandstander bent on showing up the client. The repercussions of such an action are not worth it.

An ethical problem, however, could damage your career as well as your client's. Clearing your own conscience of being an accomplice to any possible wrongdoing makes losing one client seem like small potatoes.

Understand the Environment Your Client Endures Daily

Free-lancers walk a fine line between lauding the company and commiserating with the client about the company's downsides: its lack of a day-care center, its absurd security system, overcontrol issues, or inaccessible hierarchy, for instance.

Tread delicately in sharing these kinds of conversations with your clients who endure allegedly uncomfortable, unfair, or arduous working conditions. Some clients will stoically avoid ever mentioning anything negative about their corporate life. Others will blithely chat about this and that policy, drawing you into discussions about their pros and cons. It's hard to avoid jumping into these discussions and offering opinions on the subjects.

For the sake of your business, however, fall back on listening. Inevitably the discussions turn from corporate policies themselves to the people who hand down those policies. Restrain yourself if you find you want to indulge in some people-bashing. Your client has to work with these people every day. Relationships with co-workers do wax and wane, so you don't want to find yourself on the outs with a client because you divulged some negative opinions about the client's coworker. Listen intently, offer suggestions for improving the situations, but offer no opinions about co-workers and bosses.

Learn Your Client's Personal Quirks

When launching a client relationship, learn early on what makes your client cringe or cheer about you and your work product.

Doesn't take calls before 9:30 A.M.? Never allows smoking in the office? Hates blue ink? Rarely does working lunches? Doesn't talk about private life? Hates bad grammar and spelling? Loves creative leads? Slashes quotes in leads? Likes to make small talk?

Be open to the indirect as well as the direct clues that the client dislikes something about you. If the client is fairly assertive, your job is easier. He or she will probably just come right out and tell you that you need to improve your fax machine arrangement, or that the client doesn't like your use of obscure Latin phrases in your copy, or that you can't show up even one minute late for in-house interviews.

OK. But the tougher situations are when you sense that a client doesn't like something you've done, but you can't put your finger on it. The client commented somewhat obliquely about your penchant for calling in-house sources at the end of the day. So what does that mean? Do you change your approach? Maybe.

First, why don't you think about what the reference means, whether it really is a problem, and whether you need to bring it up with the client? You don't want to sound paranoid about every little detail of your relationship, but sometimes you do need to do some maintenance.

Give your client a chance to tell you how to improve your business and your working relationship. Bring up this specific incident as an anchor for the conversation, and find out how you can change your work habits to better satisfy your client. (Learn more about post-project checkups or "postmortems" in Chapter XIII, "Revitalize Your Business.")

The Personal Life of Your Client

Occasionally, free-lancers will need to make time for a client to talk about personal issues. Because free-lancers are a nonthreatening, nonpolitical, intermittent part of the client's corporate environment, in-house personnel may feel comfortable talking about all kinds of things with them.

I devised the following interpersonal rules of the road as a derivative of my Great-grandmother Gallagher's advice: "A smart woman never talks about religion, politics, or how much money she has in her pocket." I imagine Granny Gallagher wouldn't mind if I updated her advice for both male and female audiences. My rules are:

• *NEVER charge for schmooze time.* When hard-core work discussions wind down at client meetings, sometimes small talk takes over. Just remember to account for your business time accurately and turn off your meter. You probably shouldn't halt the conversation abruptly to alert your client to your actions. But at some point, you could mention that you like to chat as much as anyone and would never charge for that time.

• *Keep political and social issues out of discussions*—unless you know for a fact that the client agrees or can laughingly disagree with you on a particular subject. One thing you never want to do is launch into a heated partisan battle that could poison your relationship.

I have several clients who do like to joust about on political issues. I try hard to stay neutral without being namby-pamby about my own opinions. One client in particular is familiar with my strong political stances and tries to goad me into discussions. Over time, we have managed to establish a humorous approach to these conversations while still tallying the latest political faux pas denied or victory claimed by one or another politician.

• *Avoid religious discussions.* This is a highly private area for most people, and I have rarely conversed with any client on matters religious. I have sometimes, however, found myself involved in discussions that have a philosophical hook. Yes, the corporate arena can inspire deep thoughts.

• *Avoid talk about how much money either of you makes.* Although your clients will know how much you're bringing in from assignments with them, don't get too specific with them about how much you gross (or net) in a year. Not only is it tacky, but you want them to think you are always hungry—no matter how much you make.

• *Help clients sort out those ubiquitous family-work juggling problems.* With so many working mothers in the corporate world, don't be surprised to have conversations about baby-sitters, day-care arrangements, and sick-child problems. And I don't mean this to sound as if it's only those working moms who launch into these subjects. Quite often I've covered the same ground with dads.

Naturally, if you're a working parent in a dual-income partnership, you probably have sorted through a few of these dilemmas and can bring some of your own solutions and anecdotes to the table. Everyone benefits from sharing this kind of information.

• *Stay away from offering marital advice.* Only once have I been in the uncomfortable position of having a client I didn't know well solicit my advice about a knotty divorce situation. I felt it inappropriate for me to give any advice or even react, and I told the client I would defer to professionals on the topic. The client understood, and our relationship continued on a less personal level.

• *Commiserate about a sickness or death.* There is no reason that you should not discuss these problems, particularly if the client brings them up. If the client is ill or in the hospital, certainly inquire about his or her status with coworkers. The same thing would apply if a client's close relative were sick or had recently died.

Certainly volunteer condolences or any other appropriate gesture (a card, flowers, or food to a funeral gathering) if you feel like doing it. Check with coworkers to see if there is something specific the family would prefer, e.g. no flowers, just donations to a particular foundation.

• *Listen intently to upcoming wedding or birth plans.* Most people in the throes of wedding or birth planning are preoccupied by the details of the upcoming events. Certainly you can spare a few minutes to hear the client's war stories or strategies. Maybe you can even share a few anecdotes dredged from your own experiences.

• *Definitely inquire about a child's or mate's activities.* When you know clients fairly well, after having worked with them several times, you will no doubt have some idea whether they are married, single, parents, divorced, or in an exclusive relationship of some sort. It's the rare corporate type who doesn't have family/child/mate photographs propped up on a bookcase somewhere.

You're certainly not hanging your keister out on a limb by inquiring about a client's family or significant others' current status and/or achievements.

Appropriate Gift-Giving

Is this just suck-up time, or can this be a real opportunity to send a sincere gesture of congratulations, season's greetings, or other sentiment to a client?

This area of the client-writer relationship can present pitfalls, unless you have genuine gift-giving motives and no expectations. The subject seems to mystify many free-lancers, who either do not want to spend the money on gifts or do not appreciate the appropriateness of the gesture.

• *Show some creativity even with traditional clients.* When choosing gifts to send to corporate clients, there's no need to stick to basics, such as flowers or food, necessarily. Actually choosing something that's a little off-center demonstrates your creativity and personality quite clearly. The gift won't just blend into the background.

So, while food or flowers are fine, use them as a platform for something more perhaps. Here's one idea: Buy avant-garde coffee mugs from a local museum and stuff them with chocolate kisses. Then place the mugs inside boxes lined not with tissue but with herbal tea bags and cocoa packets. And consider sending gifts at an offbeat time, like Valentine's Day for instance.

• *Avoid unintended double meanings with clients of the opposite sex.* By all means give your presents a personal touch, but don't bestow anything too personal like silk boxers, for example. Never give gifts that might be interpreted as off-color, sexist, racist, or suggestive in any way. This is dangerous territory, even with clients who perpetually refer to some long-running inside joke.

• *Attach simple, genuine messages to gifts.* Make an effort to let your best writing shine forth. Don't be verbose; keep it simple.

• *Use this chance to communicate with a wayward client.* All holidays, not just the winter ones, offer opportunities to send a little something to clients, especially ones with whom you haven't had much contact. They're more likely to remember your gift if you don't send it in December. Try sending something around Valentine's Day, Groundhog Day, Labor Day, or Thanksgiving instead.

• *Choose something that can be shared or taken home.* It can be more expensive to do, but so worthwhile, to send a gift or gifts that the client can share with several people, probably in the department. It's a great chance to make the gatekeepers and the bosses feel appreciated, especially if you don't have much contact with them after you've established your internal, working relationship with your client.

Chapter XII

The Networking
Necessity

Networking is a key way to get around, to get known, and to get work. It's too easy as free-lance professionals to insulate ourselves from the rest of the free world and to think of a hundred reasons not to network.

It smacks of grandstanding; there's no time; it can cost money; you could instead be doing some direct marketing or actual work; or it can mean investing off-hours time. You might rationalize that as long as you're productive, busy, and profitable, what's the rush to network?

Simply put, networking offers you exposure—something you can sorely lack if you work by yourself in a one-person organization. It's the third dimension of selling your services in a hostile business world. When you conduct your targeted marketing efforts, you're selling yourself. Every time you work with new and existing clients, you're selling yourself.

But formal and informal networking occasions let you sell yourself in a wholly different environment.

It's clear from the outset that everyone attending a networking event is there to get exposure of some sort. With that out in the open, everybody can relax a bit. Just get to know other people and build relationships. That's what it's all about. That's how you can break through barriers with in-house communicators who otherwise might not give you the time of day—even if your writing is Pulitzer stuff. It's your chance to mix, let your charisma out of the bag, and perhaps talk about what you can do and hope to do.

But these events are also your chance to back off from selling yourself so concretely, and find out who is moving and shaking the corporate communications world. This is your chance to educate yourself.

You'll meet all kinds while networking, depending on which events you attend. If the event is remotely associated with communications at corporations, you might meet:

- *Other free-lancers,* whose objectives may or may not be the same as yours. For instance, I've attended events as the guest of a client. I've also been to events and hunted down free-lancers who might subcontract assignments from me for my business.
- *In-house communications apprentices,* who can become increasingly valuable to you as they rise through the ranks. Making their acquaintance gives you layers of association within a Communications department. Remember, your client or contact will not stay in any job forever.
- *Communications decision-makers,* who naturally are key targets of your marketing efforts. However, you might consider going out of your way to avoid selling to them at these events. Once you're introduced, they'll know why you're there. If they want to talk to you about work, they will.
- *Photographers, graphics designers, and A/V producers,* who can also become allies and advertisers for your talents or collaborative skills. Regardless of whether they're in-house people or not, they can generate assignments and contacts for you.
- *Miscellaneous corporate people,* who may want to know what a free-lance writer might be able to do for them.

The Art of Schmoozing

Free-lancers need to follow several unwritten rules when attending networking organization gatherings. You will generally be in a minority at professional meetings, so you want to avoid the "foxin-the-henhouse" problem. That means that once in-house communicators know you're a free-lancer, they may be on their guard, wondering when you'll start pitching them for business.

That's why I recommend a somewhat laid-back approach to networking at professional communicators' events. You need to learn how to sell yourself subtly. Avoid the pariah label with in-house people who want to let down their hair a bit—particularly at after-work events. If they think you're on the warpath for work, they'll run as fast as they can in the other direction.

How do you avoid talking about yourself, your business, and your abilities, and actually have a productive networking session?

Talk about the other people first. Eventually they can't avoid asking about you and what brings you to a specific meeting. But bite your tongue first. Find out about them, their work, their ambitions, their background, their families, their companies. Consider these events fact-finding missions that help build your contact and friendship portfolio. All else will follow.

People like talking about themselves, their challenges, and their successes. And if you genuinely quiz them, with the intention of truly absorbing the information, they'll warm toward you and genuinely want to know about you, too. Naturally, there will be exceptions to my rule, but I've never lost out by following this approach.

Go to these events with the understanding that you're trying to expose yourself to new ideas, new communications trends, new "hot" people out there making decisions. You're building a multi-dimensional marketing exposure for yourself. You can only benefit from analyzing other people's ideas, writing styles, workplace concepts, and communications approaches.

Out and About

So how do you get this exposure if you work out of the house or a one-person office, with only a dog to fetch the mail?

While you can always market yourself through formal networking organizations, don't forget the easy, accessible strategies first:

- Lunches with clients and their in-house colleagues
- Drop-by visits to clients without extending a "sell"
- Check-in phone calls just to say hi, even if you're not on assignment with a client
- Friendly lunches with your "competition"
- Stopping by clients' coworkers' offices to drop off a note, or to say hi if you have met them before
- Checkup phone calls to contacts who almost assigned you a project or put a potential project on hold

Then there are the official ways to get out and about, by associating with or becoming a member of professional writers' organizations and professional corporate communicator organizations. These organizations' events give you and in-house communicators the chance to hook up through:

- Face-to-face interaction outside the workplace
- Business card exchanges
- Growing friendships with insiders
- Contacts that blossom into assignments
- Annual contests where writers can see how their work stacks up
- Exposure to the competition

It's one thing to become a member, but it's another thing completely to really become involved in the organization. You have to weigh your priorities and objectives. Do you want to attend events, meet people, get your name around, and develop some new business acquaintances? Or is it your intention to become critically involved in the actual nuts and bolts of the organization's operations?

That kind of involvement can require a major time commitment that you may not be able to afford. However, it can afford you an unparalleled opportunity to showcase your talents and potential value to any organization that works with you. It also might give you some face-to-face contact with corporate people who otherwise might have nothing to do with you.

Some Organizations of Note

There are many national, regional, and local communications organizations I can recommend, but you need to research which ones are most accessible to you. Once again, the public library is the place to start, to dig up phone numbers and some basics about locations, membership ranks, professional training or designation opportunities, and association membership insurance policies. Then you can just call the individual groups and have them forward membership and cost information to you.

The International Association of Business Communicators (IABC)
1 Hallidie Plaza (Suite 600), San Francisco, CA 94102
415-433-3400

Since 1970. 11,500 members worldwide. For professionals in all areas of corporate and organizational communications. IABC has an extensive library on organization communications, competitive awards, seminars, etc.

Women in Communications, Inc. (WICI, pronounced "wickee")
6211 N. Campbell Ave., Chicago, IL 60659
312-508-9424

A national organization with local and regional chapters that accommodate the networking and professional training needs of communications women.

Society for Technical Communicators
901 Stuart Street, #304, Arlington, VA 22203
703-522-4114

Since 1960. 17,000 members. For anyone engaged in or interested in some part of technical communications: companies, corporations, organizations, etc. Operates telecommunications bulletin board and produces monthly newsletter.

Associated Business Writers of America
1450 S. Havana (Suite 620), Aurora, CO 80012
303-751-7844

Since 1945. 150 members. For professional full- and part-time free-lancers who specialize in business writing. ABWA prides itself on serving as job link between editors and writers.

Public Relations Society of America
33 Irving Place, 3rd Floor, New York, NY 10003-2376
212-995-2230

Since 1947. 15,462 members. Society of public relations people in business, government, hospitals, schools, and nonprofit organizations. PRSA offers a number of professional development programs and accreditation programs.

Chapter XIII

Revitalize Your Business

Y**OUR RELATIONSHIP** with the corporate liaison can make or break your success with a given corporation, no matter how large the entity. On any assignment, you need to fulfill the company's specific wants and needs, and then make the extra effort to diagnose new ways to improve the service you provide them. This is the secret to keeping your business fresh, fulfilled, and profitable.

Even though business schools and publications hammer away at the customer focus issue, the importance of this might escape the most savvy writer, to the detriment of a client relationship. You must take an active approach to staying focused on your clients' needs and wants. Their satisfaction will control your free-lance success.

Losing a Client

Unfortunately, top-quality customer service and focus doesn't necessarily insulate you from losing a client. In spite of your best efforts, some clients will still need to suspend your services for one reason or another. Sometimes you'll finish a project and that's it for a while with a given client. Or your client liaison leaves the company, stranding you without a contact. Or a client's budget runs out. These scenarios don't suggest in any way that your services weren't up to par.

But if a good, long-standing client says adios, then you do need to analyze what went wrong. There are many possible, and sometimes intangible, reasons why you might lose a client.

One way to avoid complete relationship breakdowns is to conduct ongoing "postmortem" discussions after completing assignments. These no-charge meetings are an assertive way for you to keep open lines of communication, avoid complete disaster, and leave open the door to future work. These ongoing discussions are typically informal and not contrived. You merely conduct one after a project ends and the verdict is in about its effectiveness.

If you lose a client completely, for whatever reason, you should also consider pursuing a final postmortem discussion in the aftermath.

Staying Alive with a Postmortem

Regular postmortems, even for a one-shot assignment, allow you to inquire about your services and how you can better serve the client. It's the longer-term relationships that can be more difficult to monitor, especially if the personal and professional sides blur somewhat.

Many free-lancers endure the threat of losing a client or watching a client slough them off slowly, painfully. First, you're doing three brochures a month, then two brochures every quarter, then one every six months. Then, pretty soon they stop calling and completely brush off your inquiries about new assignments without explanation.

At that point, it's almost too late to retrieve such a client relationship. Long before this point you need to read the signs of a fading client and beef up communication in addition to conducting postmortems. Without indulging in paranoia, regularly scan your client conversations to gauge the client's satisfaction. Ask yourself the following questions:

- Is the client returning phone calls?
- Has the client decreased the amount of work you're doing?
- Has the client given you no explanations for it?
- Has the company survived the recession better than other clients, without many cutbacks or much downsizing?
- Do you see your final works completely rewritten?
- Are you surprised at the editing your client does on your work?
- Does your client avoid any additional get-togethers with you when you suggest them?
- Have you been doing more and more rewriting for your client?
- Have you noticed a lot of other free-lancers landing assignments you used to complete for the client?

Keeping Options Open

It is not necessarily curtains to lose a client, and eventually it happens to everyone. No matter how it happened, the writer still needs to consider objectively all the possible explanations:

- Sheer economics
- Change in communications strategies
- New management in communications
- The end of a one-time project
- More writing brought in-house
- Miscommunication about project parameters
- Personality conflict
- A botched assignment
- Assignment beyond your expertise

Target why you think you lost your client, then try to set up a general postmortem. This might include a discussion with the client about overall issues of your skills, versatility, attitude, and approach to assignments.

Probably the hardest part for you will be to actually pick up the phone and initiate the discussion in the first place. But it's worth it as a professional to understand thoroughly why a client won't work with you anymore. Here are some pointers on conducting a worst-case-scenario postmortem discussion with a client:

- Keep it brief.
- Retain your dignity.
- Refrain from groveling.
- Operate with as much optimism as possible.
- Listen patiently.
- Take notes.
- Summarize.
- Ask specific questions about your work and relationship.

Chin Up

A bruised ego is inevitable if you lose a client. It can be hard to face failure and criticism, but it's important to pick up and go on. The final postmortem tips above should help you put an objective spin on the situation if you can take the first step and ask the client for a final audience. This session may provide some clues to changing or adapting your writing, attitude, or approach—if not for this client, then for others.

If nothing else, at least it shows you are ultraprofessional about your business. You're asking the client's help to convert a negative into a positive for the future, even if it means not working with that client. This is one way to leave open the door, in case down the road the writer wants to reapproach the client, or in case someone else takes over that contact position.

Investing in Your Work

It can never hurt to seek a higher meaning or ambition in your work on a daily basis. It takes a real investment in creative energy, but it so benefits your clients, their companies, and whatever service or products you offer. This continual retrenching process can keep you on top of what has changed with a client company, what currently is fueling the company's productivity and profitability, and how you can better service that client.

Yes, a little passion makes this business work over the long haul.

A human being, the corporate client is a living, breathing, ever-changing entity. To keep that client-writer relationship alive, free-lancers need to refocus on all the positives that drew them together with a client in the first place and then glued them together over time. Your value will also increase as you demonstrate a consistent concern about a corporation's activities and then inject that concern into your work.

This can be done in many subtle and concrete ways. For instance, try to:

- Ask regularly what new corporate developments are in the works. Sometimes referring to a recent press article you read can lead to fascinating discussions about the company and its strategies.
- Solicit the client's opinions about specific product/service changes at the company. Talk about the effects of the company's expansions or shutdowns.
- Ask to be put on mailing lists for corporate publications you don't write.
- Ask to read any interesting archival information about the company's history. Company histories, videos, orientation materials, and films all illuminate.
- Inquire about any reorganization's effects on the client or the

Communications department. This can also clue you in to your own free-lance future, especially if new managers are coming and changing procedures.

Seeking Inspiration

You need to seek out remedies to burnout and malaise. As a free-lancer, you don't have a protective parent company sending you to creative workshops in Aspen, challenging rock-climbing retreats, or celebrity-studded writing seminars. On your own, you need to find ways to renew your creative spirit and work vitality.

Some of us fear that going away for any length of time could cost us business. Others, in a workaholic mode, cannot or will not get away from their work. And still others worry that they cannot handle a cash-flow interruption.

So what's the solution? Consider some of the "blue-sky" options for revitalizing your business and creativity, while cultivating some regular at-home habits that keep your juices pumped and clients happy.

Those options might be jogging five miles daily, meditating, or keeping a journal. Whatever you do to refuel, you need to devote some time to stoking your creative fires or you'll burn out. This chapter will offer some rationales and suggestions for a regular inspirational strategy, in the event vacations and sabbaticals are not in the cards.

If a writer, however, does want to opt for cleansing, motivational journeys, he or she can contact any of the associations listed in Chapter XII or a local university for information about writers' workshops and getaways.

You can devise your own escape from reality, but you won't experience the shared expertise and synergism of a group workshop. As with any networking event you attend, you can't help but learn something beneficial from other writing professionals at a workshop. You'll be exposed to new ideas, people, work approaches, and philosophies that you might otherwise miss.

Working by yourself, in a vacuum, with only your clients' input on your work, can stagnate your working approach and fossilize your writing. You need to get out there and discover what's happening in the free-lance corporate communications and writing world. Your clients and business can only benefit from new contributions and approaches you bring to your work.

Remember, you're always looking for new and better solutions to your clients' communications needs. It's one thing to read about those solutions, it's quite another to learn about their effectiveness firsthand from those who invented them or tried them first.

Entering the Fray

When it comes to encouraging a writer to give this business a stab, I say there's plenty of room on the playing field. Although it takes some experimentation and instinct to find the formula that works for you in landing business, understand that no one approach works for everyone attempting to succeed at this.

I hope my book gives you a more concrete, step-by-step approach to use as a starting point. Augment, merge, or compress some of my steps. Be creative, especially as you deal with more people in the business. And always, always be ready to change your approach.

As the business world changes, so must you adapt to its mutating needs and wants. You're a service provider, and you'll only be as successful at this as you are at satisfying your clients' requirements. You're also a human. And if you've adopted a bit of the maverick in your character and work approach, as many free-lancers have, that's great.

After all, that's probably what sets you apart from the rank and file anyway. You're a risk-taker who has started your own business. You're an entrepreneur who thinks that being your own boss is the most lucrative, fulfilling, and only worklife possible for you.

You're also a person who hasn't let routine douse your inspirational fires.

In the end, that's what will make you succeed as a free-lance writer for corporations. You can enter your clients' worlds and offer them a fresh, curious approach to so many products and services they may take for granted. You can make those things come alive in their corporate newsletters, videotapes, brochures, and speeches.

You can help boost morale, expand understanding among employees, convey messages of assumed responsibility, leadership, and care to the surrounding community, the shareholders, and the government.

And when you step off the company's grounds, you can know you've contributed something to the fabric of that company's being and its continued success.

Work hard, entrench yourself in each company's unique character and products, invest in your writing, absorb the people you encounter in the multifaceted work you will do. And most of all, enjoy tremendous success with this free-lance writing business.

Appendix I

"The Insiders Speak"

Results of a Communicators' Survey

I conducted a twenty-six-question multiple-choice survey of communicators at companies of various industries, sizes, and communications objectives. I have incorporated some of their comments into other parts of the book, but here I have listed the overall results of my survey.

The responses in general underlined many of my contentions about corporate communications free-lancing.

The companies ranged in size from 38 employees to 250,000 employees, with an average size of 43,213 employees. They fell into the retail, insurance, manufacturing, nonprofit, telecommunications, financial, health care, and trade association industry categories. Many of them occupy a slot in the Fortune 500.

My survey delved into the guts of free-lancers' responsibilities and relationships when they work with corporate communicators. I tried to condense into a short, multiple-choice format many of the key things that a free-lancer might want to know about how these in-house communicators think and operate.

Naturally, some of these communicators' work is dictated to them by prescribed rituals, so they may have little freedom to change policies regarding free-lancers. Others have defined their own unique game plan and strategy for choosing and dealing with free-lancers.

The Results

About 60 percent of the respondents worked in companies that centralize communications to one department. The other 40 percent were split between completely decentralized communications organizations and hybrid structures.

The companies that decentralize communications divvy up the communications functions and oversight to their operating units. The hybrid structure gives the operating units responsibility for communications but has in place a centralized, highly skilled oversight Communications department that runs corporate-wide projects and reviews operating unit projects.

So What Do They Assign to Free-lancers?

I asked respondents to name the top three types of communications projects they might have free-lancers complete.

- *Newsletters* and other employee publications tied for the lead, with 42 percent of the companies citing both in their top three free-lance assignments.
- *Speeches* were named in the top three by 32 percent of respondents.
- *Brochures* followed up with a 26 percent share.
- *Press releases and A/V scripts* grabbed a 21 percent margin.

And What Do In-House People Look at When They Consider a Free-lancer?

I asked the communicators to name the five most important credentials or characteristics a free-lancer can possess.

- Almost 90 percent of the communicators circled *portfolio/ samples* in their top five choices.
- That was followed by *referrals*, which were cited by 68 percent of the respondents.

- *Personality* came in third with a 63 percent share.
- *Journalism background* grabbed fourth with 58 percent.
- *In-house experience* was cited by 42 percent, for fifth place.

When Are Free-lancers Called?

The respondents were able to choose any or all of the six situations listed. More than 68 percent of respondents said they contract with free-lancers for *extra help with ongoing projects. Emergency projects* followed with 42 percent, and *staff shortages* were named by 32 percent as also opening up opportunities for free-lancers.

In light of this, a later question is also of interest. I asked if respondents' use of free-lancers had increased in the last couple years. While 68 percent said no, the other 32 percent said that their increased use had ranged from 10 to 75 percent over the last two years.

How About Gaining Access to an In-House Person?

Of the seven ways I suggested a free-lancer might gain business with an in-house communicator, *referrals* were identified by 84 percent of the respondents, followed by 26 percent for *letter contact*, and 15 percent for *cold calling*. The other five ways (agencies, portfolio, professional organizations, conventions, previous work) barely gained a mention.

While *hiring out-of-towners* didn't appeal to 47 percent of respondents, 32 percent said they do hire them and another 26 percent said that the decision depends on the person's background or ease of communication and access to them during assignments.

In a separate question, more than 78 percent of the in-house communicators agreed that when they're choosing a free-lancer they try to project *how well that writer will interface with their company personnel* while completing assignments. Another 11 percent said they sometimes need to do this, and only another 11 percent said they never consider this interface important.

This would make sense, because 94 percent said they let *free-lancers journey beyond the Communications department's nest* to work with other corporate personnel on assignments. Naturally, this should be a signal to a free-lancer who lacks interpersonal or appropriate interviewing skills to beef up these weaknesses.

On the Job

OK, so the free-lancer has landed an assignment with one of my survey respondents. Here is what they had to say about the ins and outs of completing assignments at their individual companies.

Long-term, the respondents spread out the votes on what they considered the three most important attributes of a free-lancer's ongoing success. For instance, *deadline adherence* pulled out 77 percent of the votes, followed by *clear writing* and *accuracy*, with 68 percent and 58 percent, respectively.

More than 42 percent said they rarely asked their contract writers for *photography support*, but another 36 percent said they sometimes ask writers to shoot a few rolls while on assignment. This certainly supports the growing idea that writers need to expand their skills beyond just the writing.

This also supports my contention that it never hurts to mention that you like to shoot production stills when on assignment. If the client gives the OK for you to shoot a few black-and-white rolls for the next publication, for instance, great. Black-and-white photography doesn't require as much sophisticated equipment or lighting as color photography does. Grated, you won't be turning out Skrebneski-quality photos (probably), but if they're decent photos, the final reproductions from a client publication will look great in your portfolio.

More than 50 percent of the respondents said they expect to *receive a disk* of the writer's completed copy, while another 31 percent expect hard copy. There was some overlap in the results here, because 36 percent also agreed they like a combination of media. Fifteen percent were in the vanguard of technologically sophisticated communicators and said they give writers the option to modem copy. As far as *how they like documents to appear*, 94 percent said they want double-spaced copy. A smattering of respondents said they look for laser-printed documents or traditional newspaper-style formatting.

It will be fascinating to see how in-house communicators handle these arrangements five or ten years from now.

Almost 80 percent of the respondents said they use *The Associated Press Stylebook*, while the rest said they adhere to the grammar and punctuation recommendations in *Merriam-Webster's Collegiate Dictionary* and *The Chicago Manual of Style*. Fifteen percent said they supplement their style checks with Strunk and White's *The Elements of Style*.

When writers come into these respondents' folds, they can expect to be *responsible for a variety of project needs*, according to 58 percent of the in-house people surveyed. Another 21 percent said they give writers only *one piece of a project*, while the other 21 percent said they will dish out *all the writing* for a project.

Generally these communicators operate on pretty tight *deadlines*. More than 42 percent said they have only one to two weeks for projects to be completed. Twenty-one percent admitted to elastic deadlines. And when you turn in your copy, 52 percent said they will have contracted for a *rough draft and one rewrite*. The next biggest group contracts for a *draft and two rewrites*, and 10 percent expect *perfect first drafts*.

And, the group was split between preferring a *straight/newsy* style and a *colorful/feature* style of writing.

When you come on board to write an assignment, you generally won't be left to your own *research devices*. More than 84 percent of these in-house communicators said they give you *any/all printed materials* they have available related to your subject. Seventy-nine percent said they will give you sources' *phone numbers*, 31 percent said they will write up *outlines* for you, another 31 percent said they will *pre-interview sources* for you, and 10 percent said they will *attend the interviews* with you.

Let's Talk Money

More than 42 percent of the group said they like to name a *set fee* for projects, 21 percent said they like to work in *hourly rates*, and another 31 percent said they will *negotiate* the fees and rates per project.

Half of the in-house communicators who work with hourly rates said they will negotiate different rates for different projects. Another 26 percent said they will pay between $65 and $85 per hour. Another 16 percent said they will pay between $45 and $65 per hour, and a small number said they pay free-lancers up to $125 an hour.

On the subject of *expenses*, 90 percent said they will pay messenger/express mail fees, 80 percent said they will pay travel expenses, and 64 percent said they will pay phone expenses. Forty-two percent said they will pay commuting/mileage costs, and the same percent said they will pay for faxes. A smattering said they will pay for supplies.

Keeping a Client

If you're curious what can cause an in-house communicator to *sever a relationship with a free-lancer*, the respondents were quite firm in their answers, sometimes circling all my seven suggested reasons.

All respondents agreed that *shoddy work* was the top reason for showing a free-lancer the door. *Deadline problems* and *personality conflicts* came in second, as cited by 79 percent of respondents. Fifty-eight percent of the respondents thought that *ethical problems* meant curtains. *Hiring a full-time communications staffer, a decreased communications budget*, and *coming in over budget* each were circled by 31 percent.

The Analysis

All in all, I wasn't surprised by the results of the survey. However, I was glad to see so many of my factual and intuitive assumptions about free-lancing supported by the vast majority of respondents.

In general, I avoided surveying my own clients, so as not to skew any results. The few who did respond offered objective and consistent answers akin to all the others.

I hope that this raw data gives other free-lancers a more clear idea of what in-house communicators expect from them—in the marketing phase, the assignment phase, the fee negotiation phase, and during the ongoing tenure of the free-lancer's in-house relationship.

Some of my own experiences and advice diverge from some of the above results, probably because there is no hard-and-fast formula for gaining and keeping corporate free-lance business.

As Larry Robbins, the director of the Communications program for the Wharton School, said, "This whole area of communications is subject to change constantly. And, until now, so little of its merits have been quantified that anything is possible when it comes to finding this kind of in-house free-lance work."

Appendix II

Stylebooks and Grammar References

The Associated Press Stylebook. Norm Goldstein, editor. New York: The Associated Press, 1994. *My first source for style points.*

The Columbia Guide to Standard American English Usage. New York: The College University Press, 1993. *An interesting update of many old and new style points.*

Fowler, Henry, and Fowler, F. G. *A Dictionary of Modern English Usage.* Oxford: Oxford University Press. *A huge tome; a valuable investment for any writer.*

Kipfer, Barbara. *The Twenty-First-Century Manual of Style.* New York: Dell Press, 1993.

Merriam-Webster's Ninth New Collegiate Dictionary. Springfield, MA: Merriam-Webster, Inc., 1983, principal copyright date. *My definitive spelling source and tiebreaker for other style debates.*

Strunk, William, and White, E. B. *The Elements of Style.* New York: Macmillan Publishing Co., Inc., 1979. *A slim but critical standby for any writer.*

Appendix III

Tax Reference Books

Here is a list of tax books you can refer to. I understand they are updated regularly.

Consumer Reports Books. *Guide to Income Tax 1994 Edition.* Yonkers, New York: Consumer Reports Books, A Division of Consumer's Union. 730 pages, softcover, oversize. *This guide includes a chapter entitled "Taking Care of Business." The publishers also produce a tax workbook with all the latest 1994 information.*

Ernst and Young. *The Ernst & Young Tax Guide 1994.* Peter W. Bernstein, editor. New York: John Wiley & Sons, Inc. 732 pages, softcover, oversize. *This tome includes a chapter entitled "Self-Employed Entrepreneur's Tax Guide," and is an official IRS tax guide.*

Lasser, J. K. *Your Income Tax 1994.* New York: Prentice Hall. 511 pages, softcover, oversize. *This is a guide to the new tax changes in effect and includes sample forms and instructions.*

Sprouse, Mary L., with the editors of *MONEY* magazine. *The MONEY 1994 Income Tax Handbook.* New York: Warner Books. *With 650 pages, plus forms, I would hardly call this a handbook, but it appears to have a lot of easy-to-understand explanations of tax issues. It even claims to be the "easiest and most complete guide."*

Index

About the Author

Maryclaire Collins launched her free-lance corporate communications business in 1986, armed with a journalism master's degree from the Medill School of Journalism at Northwestern University, three years in video production, and two years in public relations at a Fortune 500 company.

Her clientele has included Kraft General Foods, the Amoco Corporation, Allstate Insurance, Ameritech, FMC Corporation, Zurich-American Insurance Group, Citicorp, CNA Insurance, Chicago's METRA transit system, Price Waterhouse, Vanguard Construction, Motivation Media, Inc., Whirlpool, and Blue Cross/Blue Shield of Illinois.

She refines her successful business and marketing strategies from the "war room" of her Highland Park, Illinois, home, with the support of her husband, two children, and two loyal but unskilled canines. Now she's ready to share what she has learned with other writers who want to try their luck at free-lance writing for corporations.